Voices of CHANGE

2-Minute Inspirational Stories on Life's Lessons Learned

KATHY LYNN

VOICES OF CHANGE

2-Minute Inspirational Stories on Life's Lessons Learned

by

Kathy Lynn

GATSBY

PUBLISHING

Published by:
Gatsby Publishing
301 Delaronde Street
New Orleans, LA 70114-USA
www.kathylynn.net

Printed in the United States of America
First Printing: 2009

Cover design by TLW Productions
Book design by TLW Productions

Library of Congress Control Number: 2009907242
ISBN: 978-0-9824079-1-2

What people are saying about *Voices of Change:*

In *Voices of Change*, Kathy Lynn captures an amazing number of unique stories from individuals just like you and me – stories with which we all can identify. Each of us is unique, and if the world doesn't hear our stories, it will not know how we lived our lives. All you have to do is read Kathy's Table of Contents to know she has captured most of the paths we've all followed. At the end of each story, she offers "learnings" from that story. Kathy's book is a must-read for all of us who want to savor our own memories of how we lived our lives.

Ed Poole, Author: *Lessons from the Porch: A Gathering Place for Telling Our Stories, Lessons from the Crossroads: Finding My Authentic Path, and Lessons from Empowering Leaders: Real Life Stories to Inspire Your Organization Toward Greater Success*
Boone, NC

Let Kathy Lynn's *Voices of Change* introduce you to ordinary people who met extraordinary challenges with heroism, leadership and grace.

Chastian "Choose" Taurman III, Director of Business Studies at Tulane University
New Orleans, LA

Life can be anything we want it to be if we learn from the experiences that come our way every day. *Voices of Change* can be your own personal how-to guide on dealing with life changes – the ones we choose, and the ones that are thrust upon us.

Jim Tucker, Speaker of the Louisiana House of Representatives
Baton Rouge, LA

Her vignettes are believable. Her solutions are even more refreshing. This work is more of a manual for life than a compilation of life experiences. Enlightening, uplifting and rewarding. Oprah! Be sure and read this one!

Juan Enrique Coleman III, Investor with Cima Estelar
Costa Rica

In the 17 years that I have known Kathy Lynn, she has been an outstanding leader and always committed to change. How appropriate for her book to be an advocacy for the same. This is a collection of stories about events that impacted individuals to make dramatic change in their lives. Most timely and appropriate!

Rick Doran, President, People First Consultants;
Author of *Twelve Steps to Customer Trust*
Indianapolis, IN

Voices of Change will be an inspiration to anyone who refuses to give up and has the heart to review and change their lives for the better. I like the format that you have established, and the stories grab the reader's interest. I can't wait until the book comes out. Best of luck on a surefire hit!

Dr. Donna Alley, Provost & Professor, Delgado Community College
New Orleans, LA

This book *Voices of Change* is one that speaks to the heart and soul of all of us. These true stories show us how resilient we can be when we are committed to rising above our circumstances and manifesting what we say we want. Thank you Kathy Lynn for lighting our path once again.

Lisa LeBlanc, Business Coach and Consultant, Creative Team Design
New Orleans, LA

Kathy, as you know, I have written a book and was fortunate to have it be a best seller. I have also had the opportunity to read some good nonfiction in my day. I must tell you that your book brought out in me all of the feelings that I require from a good read. I found myself crying and laughing all at the same time. I felt fear and compassion and joy. Your book is fabulous and is an inspiration! You go, girl!

Gennifer Flowers, Singer, Author, Comedienne and Columnist
New Orleans, LA

Far from being a how-to book, *Voices of Change* is a collection of beautiful and mesmerizing tales of the surprising fulfillment in life changes. Devoid of sensationalism and simplistic generalizations, it tells the real stories of real people who have found their way through devastating circumstances and life-altering choices to make a change into lives that are richer and filled with meaning. Candidly honest, Kathy Lynn has given us delightful glimpses into what change can bring!

Leah Henderson, Leah Henderson & Associates, Business and Life Coach
Atlanta, GA

One can never get too much inspiration in life. Kathy Lynn has compiled stories that will have you clapping your hands and shouting "Yes!" to the resilience, courage and persistence of these voices of change!

Dr. Vikki Ashley, author of *How to Be A BITCH With Style: Being in Total Control of Herself*; and *Alan's Song of Love: Our AIDS Odyssey*
New Orleans, LA

ACKNOWLEDGEMENTS

Voices of Change is dedicated to:

My mother and best friend, O'Dear, who was as wonderful and unique a person as her name – truly one of a kind. She was always there for me, and she always believed that I could do anything in life that I set my mind to. She made me believe it, too. Thank you, Mom.

To my adopted mother and one of the strongest, most compassionate and caring women I have ever had the pleasure of knowing, "Ms. Irene" Burrus. She has taught me, by the example she sets daily, how important it is to take time to make others feel special.

A heartfelt thank you goes to the following people, without whose help this book never would have been written: Fay Faron, my weekly book coach and author of five books; Dr. Vikki Ashely, my monthly coach and a bestselling author and motivational speaker; Ed Poole, my quarterly coach, talk-radio host and author, who gave me direction when I didn't know what to do or where to go during the process; and to Hollie Vest, my close friend, international entertainer and owner of Magnolia Mansion in New Orleans, who always motivates me and believes in me.

Thank you to the following friends who helped with introductions, ideas, editing and motivation: Ken Graham, Marcia Ensley, Jerri Taylor, Marty Broussard, Fritz Harsdorff, Tim Weston, Lisa LeBlanc, Paul Richardson, Nan Charpiot and Wendy Lea.

To the friends who influenced my life with their leadership and caring: Joe McFadden, Bob Clemens, Dwight Hammack, Chuck Martin, Mike Simpson, Tim Plohg, and my sister, Donna Sue.

I am also grateful to the wonderful team at TLW Productions for the superb product, guidance, hand-holding and encouragement from the beginning to the end of the project.

A special thank you goes to the incredible people who have allowed me to share their stories. I deeply appreciate the life lessons learned from each.

To the love in my life, Lucien Andrew Landry, for the love, peace and happiness he brings me daily.

Thank you to all of my other friends and neighbors who make my life so special.

And finally, thank you, Lord, for all of the above and for my life and the lessons learned.

CONTENTS

INTRODUCTION

Everyone has a story to tell. I had been trying to tell mine for seven years, but I was experiencing so much life change that I couldn't slow down long enough to tell it.

In seven short years I was divorced, fell in love again, moved, changed careers after twenty-four years, started two businesses and lost one of them. I also lost my mom, my dad, and my beloved four-legged best friend - the Gatsby Dog, and I experienced Hurricane Katrina, the largest disaster ever to hit the United States.

I now realize that these life-changing events prepared me to write my book and enabled me to relate more fully to the people whose stories I would be telling. I have also included a few of my own stories.

That is what *Voices of Change* is all about - change and the lessons it imparts as we go through this journey called life. These lessons can apply to both our professional and personal lives.

This book contains stories on every aspect of life, from death, divorce and career changes, to life changes, sex-life changes, and spiritual changes. I didn't set out with a particular number in mind or a specific type of interview I wanted to conduct. The right people with a story to tell just seemed to show up at the right time. Of course, I am a firm believer that people come and go in our lives precisely when they are supposed to.

As you read these short stories about change, I hope you are as inspired as I was when I conducted the interviews. Each one was a learning experience for me, personally. At the end of every story, the storyteller shares what he or she learned through the experience of change. I dedicated a final chapter to a compilation of those thoughts.

Also, at the end of each chapter I included some questions that I hope will provoke thought and inspire readers to make the changes they desire in their own lives.

So enjoy the lessons learned. It is my hope that they can help you live your life to the fullest as you go through your own journey.

Kathy Lynn

If you would know the road ahead, ask someone who has traveled it.
–Chinese Proverb

LESSON 1

UNDERSTAND WHAT LIFE IS ABOUT AND HOW YOU FIT IN

"Happiness does not depend on outward things, but on the way we see them."

Leo Tolstoy

Hurricane Katrina Teaches Gratitude

Lesson: *"No woulda, shoulda, coulda for me."*

–Angela Cryer, Social Worker
Married to Police Officer for 24 Years
New Orleans

Angela had lived next door to her parents for her entire married life before Hurricane Katrina, and she loved the feeling of an extended family. But that all changed when both houses took on twelve feet of floodwater.

The Saturday before the storm hit, Angela's husband, Reginald, sent her to get extra supplies. The next day, the couple and their two sons saw the televised warnings from city officials and decided it was time to get the family out. Angela had always known that if the time came, Reginald, a New Orleans police officer for more than twenty years, would stay. It was his duty to take care of others. But she never imagined the nightmarish days that would follow, when she wouldn't know if he was dead or alive.

It took Angela and her family twelve hours to make what is normally a one-hour drive to her brother's house in the city of Baton Rouge. Angela was in constant touch with Reginald, and after the storm moved ashore Monday she spoke to him by phone. He told her that everything in New Orleans was just fine, and that she should able to bring the kids home in a couple of days.

Suddenly, while they were talking, Reginald told Angela that he had to hang up because something big was happening. What Reginald was witnessing was the water rising rapidly on Napoleon Avenue, one of the city's larger thoroughfares. He drove quickly to a raised parking garage at nearby Memorial Hospital, where he and many others would be stranded for days without food, water, supplies, power or communications.

Angela and her family watched in shock with the rest of the world as the terror of Katrina unfolded. There were reports of police being shot, and Angela could only imagine the worst. There was no communication in or out of the city.

When I interviewed her, Angela told me how grateful she was that her employer, Goodwill Industries, kept her and her co-workers busy during those difficult days. The organization put them to work in a Goodwill store in Baton Rouge helping other people. Angela said it was quite an experience to go from working in an executive office in downtown New Orleans, where she helped people find jobs, to helping people with basic necessities. It gave her an appreciation for the other side of the business.

It would be five days before Angela got a phone call from Reginald telling her that he was ok. He had made his way to the Second District police station, where officers were living in grim conditions. But he was alive. Alive and missing her.

It would be two and a half more weeks before Angela saw her husband – the longest they had ever been separated. Carnival Cruise Lines dedicated two cruise ships to housing first-responders in New Orleans. Angela was able to come to the city and live with Reginald on the cruise ship on weekends, but she had to return to Baton Rouge to work during the week.

Angela became very animated when she described the day she saw Reginald for the first time after the storm. She said it was like a scene from a Hollywood movie. Just to touch him was heaven. They ran into each other's arms and didn't let go for a long time. She said it was like seeing him for the very first time. They are now more in love than ever, and their relationship has grown stronger in every way.

But she said it was stressful having to live in two places at once and trying to keep the family together and the boys in school. After a while, they were able to rent a house, but the area was practically unpopulated and there were no working streetlights. All of the stores closed at 5 p.m. There were no after-school activities for the boys, so Angela made every effort to have a family dinner each night. During the meal they would talk about the storm and about life, and Angela said they became closer as a result of the experience. Most of all, though, Angela missed having her mom and dad next door. New Orleans was truly a dysfunctional city at that point. Nothing was normal, no matter how hard they tried. But Angela's faith and family got her through it.

The couple had lost their home and all of their belongings, but they had each other, their sons and Angela's parents, and that was what mattered most. Although they missed the family photos, they came to realize that material objects are not really important at all in life. It's the people who matter most.

Angela said the storm gave her a better life because she now sees things through a new set of eyes. The most valuable thing she has learned is the importance of giving back. She told me she didn't understand until after the storm why we are all here. Now, it is very clear to her. The experience of being on the other side of the desk and seeking help herself brought it all home. We are here to help others.

"I want to be there for others and give back to them like they helped me and my family," Angela said.

Angela has since joined the NO/AIDS Board of Directors, she volunteers at her church, and she mentors young people. Angela said she knows she will be gone one day, but if she helps younger people now, maybe they will help others.

Learnings:

- Angela learned patience and forgiveness. If she gets mad now, she gets over it quickly. Life is too short, and tomorrow is not promised.
- It is possible for relationships to grow stronger in the face of adversity. Angela's marriage has grown, and she and her husband have grown as friends. They say I love you more often and call each other several times a day just to say hello.
- Angela grew spiritually and learned the value of volunteering and helping others. She thought about how she was helped, and vowed to give back.
- Angela has learned not to make excuses. Don't put anything off. Don't wait until tomorrow, because tomorrow may not come. Truly live in the moment.
- No "woulda, coulda, shoulda" in Angela's book anymore. Just do it!

Each Lesson Prepares Us For Living

Lesson: *"The moments in which we have challenges are the ones from which we learn. Whether tragic or positive, it is when we are pushed that we learn and grow."*

–B.B. St. Roman, Former Documentary Sound Artist and Current Executive Director for the New Orleans Police Department's Homeless Assistance Program

In the late 1960s B.B. St. Roman moved from Kentucky to New York City, where she became a documentary film sound recordist. During the 1970s and 80s she traveled with film crews to such exotic places as Asia, South America and Africa to document the lives of people such as Mother Teresa, the Dalai Lama, the shamans of the Himalayas, African tribal chieftains, and many more. From 1983 to 1993 she worked as the road manager for New Orleans musician Dr. John. B.B. has had a full life and has learned much

along the way. Her many experiences in starkly different regions of the world and among various spiritual leaders prepared her for her current position in life – caring for the homeless of New Orleans through the New Orleans Police Department.

B.B.'s most intense documentary adventure took her to the Himalayas to film the rituals of the shamans in remote parts of Nepal. After their plane landed, she and her crew traveled by car along winding mountain roads for one long day until the roads ended and they had to get out and walk. They hiked for seven days to reach the village they had chosen for their work. The crew traveled to that village three different times, staying each time for three months. After that, B.B. went back to visit twice.

The village had little contact with the outside world and no modern conveniences. While the rest of the team pitched tents and lived on the outskirts, B.B. decided to immerse herself in the culture. She rented a simple hut with a dirt floor and no furniture. In fact, no one in the village had furniture – no tables, chairs or beds. Instead, a single blanket served all purposes: folded up it was a seat, spread out it was a bed, and wrapped around the shoulders it was a coat. Their meals each day consisted of corn mush and sometimes a spinach-like plant, eaten with the hands because there were no forks or spoons. A fire was kept burning at all times because the villagers needed it for heat, light and cooking. There were no matches, no kerosene lanterns, no candles, no stoves. The fire was everything. There also were no bathrooms – only the cow stalls or the nearby cornfields.

Between filming sessions, B.B. picked barley, carried river water on her back, and learned the shamanic ways. The shamans were the healers called to the homes of sick people to perform elaborate rituals. All sickness was thought to be a separation of the spirit from the body, either caused by one's own neglect or by a spell from a

negative person, living or dead. The shamans would heal the sick person by drumming, dancing, singing and going into trance to call the spirit back. Sometimes the spirit of the sick person had separated itself too far from the body, and the shamans could not retrieve it. It was beyond their control, and they would accept it.

The songs and rituals used for healing were passed down from generation to generation. New shamans were called into service by ancestor shamans who entered their bodies and caused them to shake, passing on to them the power to communicate with the spirit world. The new shaman then had the duty to henceforth serve the community as a healer.

Living among the shamans changed B.B. dramatically. The shamans had accepted her and wanted her to participate in their rituals. They gave her a drum to play and taught her their songs. They said she should take this understanding of the spirit world back home with her to help heal people. Staying among the highest mountains in the world gave B.B. a new inner strength. She felt the experience empowered her to take on anything.

After her third stay with the shamans, B.B. found out what the experience had prepared her for when her flight from Kathmandu landed in New York. A friend met her at the airport and told her that her parents had just been killed in Kentucky, and that she had a ticket to fly on to Louisville. B.B. said she realized that her lessons in the Himalayas had happened for a reason, and at just the right time, to prepare her. She was ready to accept and deal with losing her parents so tragically because she had learned that there is a spiritual level to life that we may not understand, but which we must respect. Events happen on that level that we cannot control, and they happen for their own reasons and in their own time. B.B. knew she needed to remain calm and strong like a mountain, and appreciate all the time she had spent with her parents and all the wonderful lessons they had taught her.

Later, B.B. returned to the areas of Nepal, India and Sikkim for more documentary filming, and to get a different spiritual experience – that of being with the Dalai Lama and the Tibetan Buddhists. Their teachings are focused on wisdom. They feel that you change the world by changing yourself, and that your attitude toward life determines how life treats you. If you treat others with the highest respect, like a Buddha, you will receive respect. If you seek happiness for other people, you will always be happy yourself. Also, depending on your attitude, you create your own Heaven or Hell on earth.

Another important Buddhist teaching is that life is always changing; it is never permanent. In one documentary B.B. worked on, the Buddhist monks created an intricate mandala, consisting of beautiful geometric patterns made with different colors of sand. They worked on their creation nonstop for two weeks. Then, on the full moon, the head Lama poured all of the sand into a jar and then sprinkled it into a stream that ran down the mountainside to the rest of the world. The monks had taken the energy they put into the mandala and changed it into a form they could pass on to the rest of the world.

After her parents passed away, B.B. found a new "spiritual mother" and "spiritual father." B.B. was called to record the sound for a film documenting the life of Mother Teresa, and B.B. ended up traveling extensively with her off and on for two years. Mother Teresa taught by example: She openly showed love and respect for each person she came into contact with, and she consistently put her love into action. One day she was speaking before the United Nations; the next day she was scrubbing a crib for a baby. Whatever needed to be done, Mother Teresa would do it. She felt that if she helped one person, it was enough, but if she could help more, so

much the better.

B.B. describes Dr. John as her "spiritual father." She spent ten years as his road manager, and never once did he command her to "do this or that." He was never in a hurry or stressed out, and he taught B.B. to relax and enjoy handling the details of being on the road with a full band. Like Mother Teresa, Dr. John showed respect for every person, but especially for the little guy. When eating out, Dr. John seemed more interested in meeting the cook who prepared his food than the owner of the restaurant. He also had plenty of spiritual teachings to pass on. He gave B.B. a quote that she still uses today: "You have to be in season in order to catch the season when it comes."

Both Mother Teresa and Dr. John opened B.B.'s eyes to the need for compassion for others. And all of these people – the shamans, the Dalai Lama, Mother Teresa and Dr. John – displayed a special sense of happiness that comes from tranquility and contentment of the inner spirit. B.B. believes that all of her varied experiences prepared her for her current job working with the homeless in New Orleans. She said she considers this work her most important contribution to date.

Learnings:

- Three things matter most in life: wisdom – understanding what life is about and how you fit in and set your priorities; compassion – showing feeling and respect for others; and joy – inner contentment that leads to the outer expression of happiness.
- It is possible to get along with very few material comforts, as B.B. learned by living in a Himalayan village and in many other locations around the world.
- Patience is a great virtue, especially in situations beyond your control. One might as well enjoy the situation instead of getting upset about it. Traveling to other countries teaches patience quickly!

- Resilience is important – knowing how much you can endure and stretching that boundary further.
- Learn to go with the flow, knowing that everything happens for a reason and at the right time, even if we don't immediately understand it.
- Accept what you have in life and enjoy it.
- Draw from nature to be resourceful. B.B. learned resourcefulness from watching the villagers in the Himalayas work in harmony with their surroundings. There was no calendar, so the moon was used to mark the passing of days. Distance was measured in the days it took to walk somewhere.
- The rhythms of nature are all around us. We can see them in our own backyard if we simply take the time to look.

Naked Before God

Lesson: *"Lose the guilt in your life, whatever it is."*

–Jane, Program Director for Non-Profit
New Orleans

After Hurricane Katrina, Jane had an epiphany. Guilt. Jane was feeling such guilt each day after the storm when she returned to work as a counselor. While listening to people talk about their material losses and about losing loved ones, Jane felt guilty about being so lucky. She also felt guilt for having a horrible sense of loss, even though she suffered no material losses. While she did not lose personal belongings or people she loved, she lost her city, and it finally came to her one day: She was going through the same grieving process as the people she was counseling.

How did the people she talked to each day, the ones who had lost everything in their lives, have such a sense of hope? She realized that she was missing something. She plodded through most days feeling numb.

One man's story really affected her. The man told Jane about losing family and friends and all of his possessions. And then he said he would go through it again if given the choice. When Jane asked him why, he said that once he had no title, no material possessions and no status, it was just him. He had lost everything that defined who he was, but he found himself in the process.

As the days went by, Jane felt she was suffocating. She realized that she wasn't dealing with her own issues, one of which was dissatisfaction with her marriage. She described her epiphany as "standing naked before God." When you suffer loss, it forces you to examine not just your circumstances, but your very soul. Jane was counseling people who had lost it all, but who still had a spark that propelled them to go forward. Jane asked herself – what was this about?

"I felt like a hypocrite," she said. "I was helping and coaching others, but I wasn't facing my own unhappiness. I decided to start living what I was preaching every day."

Jane began making changes, and one of them was a decision to separate from her husband and move to a new neighborhood.

"I am allowing myself to be who I am, and I'm getting to know myself," she said.

Jane said the separation has improved the relationship. Now when she talks with her husband, she feels he really listens to her. She also understands him better. Jane feels she is on a journey of self-discovery, and she believes God gave her the courage to do it.

Learnings:

- Jane learned that we are all connected as a community. She realized that everyone who experienced Hurricane Katrina lost something because of the way we are all connected.
- Stay in the present and savor the moment.

- Give people your full attention and respect.
- Get angry and let it out, but don't wallow.
- Lose the guilt in your life, whatever it is.

You Have To Work At Marriage To Keep It Going

Lesson: *"Marriage is an unnatural state."*
–Jo and Fritz Harsdorff, Married 56 Years
New Orleans

"Marriage is an unnatural state," Fritz said as I sat down to interview him and his wife, Jo. She quickly quipped back: "We've been married for fifty-six years, and we're still not sure it's going to work out."

It was immediately apparent that a sense of humor has served this couple well. It has seen them through the adoption of three children, the loss of one, bouts of illness and life's usual ups and downs.

Fritz and Jo met at the local newspaper in Corpus Christi, Texas. They said when they look back, they don't know how they made it through that first year together. They were barely hanging on financially and had to take out several bank loans to make ends meet, even though they were both employed full-time at the paper. They were very proud that they never had to borrow from their families or ask them for help.

Fritz and Jo said their one-day-at-a-time philosophy has allowed the right things to happen at the right times. They are now retired, financially secure and happy, and they feel that their lives were planned by a higher power. The couple said that if you just stay out of your own way, you are usually better off. Stay open to change and guidance from others, and have a strong sense of your

own wants and needs.

About four years into their relationship, Fritz was offered a job in New Orleans, and the couple settled in the French Quarter on Chartres Street. They thought they'd stay a couple of years and return to Texas, but as Fritz described it: "The culture here just grabs you, and you can never leave it."

Jo also landed a job, and they had such fun living the French Quarter life and walking to work each day. Their house was the "party house" for their newspaper coworkers, who became their extended family in New Orleans. To this day, that hasn't changed. Neighbors still come daily for coffee and conversation with these two delightful, charming people. Fritz eventually became the associate news editor for the New Orleans newspaper.

When they adopted three children, they divided up the household responsibilities – with Fritz doing the cooking – so Jo could pursue a new career in real estate. It was a team effort that allowed them to raise their children. Jo's sales talent propelled her to the top five percent of agents in the New Orleans area. Fritz said her career strengthened her identity and made her incredibly happy.

But life was not always rosy. Fritz described a period when Jo left him and took the kids to Texas for nine months. He said he missed her and the children each day they were gone, and he knew he couldn't live without them. She felt the same way. As they told this story, they looked at each other with a deep love that is still vibrant fifty-six years later. Jo told me how it lifts her heart each morning when she hears Fritz whistle as he comes down the stairs.

"Where has the time gone?" they both wondered. Fifty-six years had flown by.

Today, Jo and Fritz enjoy their grandchildren and great-grandchildren, and they still entertain the extended family on weekends and holidays. Their house is truly the neighborhood gathering place, made warm and inviting by two people blessed to have each other.

Learnings:

- You have to work at marriage to keep it strong.
- Be tolerant of your partner's faults.
- Make a commitment to the marriage, and no matter what, work it out. If one person is down, the other picks up the slack. Be a constant best friend and partner.
- Love and respect one another at all times.
- Become comfortable with each other.
- Separate bedrooms are a must. This arrangement allows each person privacy and space.
- Too much togetherness is a blow to any marriage. You must have freedom and absolute trust.
- A sense of humor is essential.
- It's important to truly like each other as friends.
- Love where you live.

His Life's Work Is Meaningful Because It Brings Joy To Others

Lesson: *"God gave us all a talent, and we need to pursue it with passion and enthusiasm every day we're alive."*

–Blaine Kern, "Mr. Mardi Gras"
New Orleans

I couldn't believe my ears when I interviewed the man who is considered the Walt Disney of New Orleans. Blaine Kern, or "Mr. Mardi Gras," as he is known around the world, told me one of the

biggest changes in his life was a change in his attitude about the value of his work.

Blaine, now eighty-one, has been building floats, hosting parades and simply making people smile since he was a little boy. As a child, he said he never really fit in and seemed to march to a different drummer. New Orleans is grateful that he continues to do so.

Blaine's one true love, aside from his family, is his work. He describes himself as married to it. Early on in his career, Blaine was offered a job by Walt Disney, but he declined. He and Walt remained friends, and Blaine's work has since expanded to venues across the country, including Universal Studios. Whenever and wherever a parade is being planned or Mardi Gras is being celebrated, his company, Blaine Kern's Mardi Gras World, is sure to be involved.

It wasn't until about ten years ago that Blaine felt his work was good enough to be considered real art, and he realized then that he would be remembered for it long after he was gone. A life-changing conversation with a dear friend helped Blaine see that his creations are both important and inspirational. Blaine's art makes people happy. As his floats roll down the streets with their larger-than-life, colorful forms, the smiles they bring to adults and children alike are invaluable.

That conversation convinced Blaine that his gift was his ability to bring happiness into the lives of others. His art will be remembered forever as each generation continues to celebrate the Carnival season.

Blaine's realization also encouraged his philanthropy. Blaine has adopted schools and other organizations around the state and city. He has hosted countless fund-raisers and benefits for good causes. He opened his facility, Mardi Gras World, just days after Hurricane Katrina, and he teamed up with the military and federal officials to provide ice and water to thousands of people.

Blaine has given so much to the city he loves, and he has become a great ambassador for New Orleans.

Learnings:

- Blaine learned from and inherited his father's talent for storytelling. Storytelling is part of being creative and passing life's lessons to the next generation.
- Cultivate the Taurus spirit of never giving up on any task you undertake – business or personal.
- Keep a positive attitude and have enthusiasm for everything you do.
- Stay physically active. Drink in moderation.
- Be able to laugh at yourself.
- Find what you were meant to do in life and pursue it relentlessly.

My Purpose In Life

Lesson:

"We should never stop learning and changing. That is the secret to living your life to the fullest.
–Kathy Lynn

I think as we get older – whatever age that is – it is natural for us to start to reflect on what we have accomplished in our lives and what is still to be done.

I believe God put each of us here for a purpose, and it unfolds over our lifetime. Some of us find that purpose early on, while others bloom later. Maybe it's volunteering to help others. Maybe it's the gift of being able to play beautiful music. Maybe it's being an artist or author or running your own company. Or maybe it's being a mother and raising beautiful, happy children.

As I examine my own life, I see the different roles that I've played. I've been daughter, friend, sister, wife, aunt, business executive, business consultant and entrepreneur. I think all of these roles were in preparation for my next step in life, which I believe is slowly being revealed.

I must digress for a moment. When I was with the company where I spent much of my career, I did a lot of public speaking, sometimes to employees and their guests. It could be a group of sixty at a local function or a group of eight hundred at a large Las Vegas conference. I also spoke to business groups and was asked by different organizations to deliver motivational speeches. I always loved this part of my job, and I was energized by the act of planning the speech and then delivering it and seeing how people responded.

When I left the company to start my own business, people just assumed that I would eventually have a full-time career as a public speaker. But for whatever reason, I never pursued it. They say that if you ask five people who know you well what you are best at, their answers will probably reveal something about your purpose in life. I should have listened earlier. But then, things happen when they are supposed to. That is my belief.

When I started writing this book, it was something I had been wanting to do for several years. I wanted to add being a published author to my list of accomplishments. But now I realize that the book is just part of my role. I also have a desire to speak publicly, sharing the stories and message of my book with groups large and small. And I also think I'm meant to speak to people about God's influence in my life. I'm still examining how that will unfold, but I know that additional books and public speaking will be part of my future. And that makes me very happy.

I have a wonderful career and I enjoy working. But more

importantly, I feel that I am pursuing what I was meant to do in life. I believe this journey is the real source of peace and joy. We should never stop learning and changing. That is the secret to living your life to the fullest.

Learnings:

- Listen to what people say you are good at. It may reveal your life's purpose.
- Embrace life changes. There is a master plan for each of us, and by changing we are getting closer to what we are meant to do.

Lesson 1 Questions

What are your personal beliefs about life and how you fit in?

What one belief could you examine to enrich your life or make your life fuller?

LESSON 2

BE TRUE TO YOURSELF, NO MATTER WHAT

"Ye shall know the truth, and the truth shall make you free."

Bible, John: 8:32

From Nurse To
Full-Time Musician

Lesson: *"No matter what happens when you try something new, it's not the end of the world if it doesn't work out. And it's better to have tried it and be able to say you did, than to never try at all."*
–Amanda Overmyer, "American Idol" Contestant

The above is good advice from a young nurse who rides a Harley and sings rock-and-roll music. In fact, when I interviewed Amanda, I felt I was speaking with someone who had lived much longer than her twenty-three years. I think it's her self-confidence and her certainty about what she wants in life that give her the air of being much older and more experienced.

Before 2008, Amanda worked as a nurse and performed her music on the weekends. At her shows, people would often approach her and tell her she should try out for "American Idol" or go to Los Angeles and try to break into the music scene there. But Amanda said she never felt she had the time. In addition to her full-time job, she was working to complete her bachelor's degree in business management. Anyway, she said, "American Idol" was a pop show. They would never choose someone like her – a rocker who rides a motorcycle.

But then she began to think about it. Amanda is a risk-taker, or – as she told me – she takes calculated risks. She said she realized she had nothing to lose by auditioning for the show. She could always return to being a nurse. She said the trip to the Atlanta auditions was made on a whim when she had some time off and felt she could afford to give it a shot. In fact, she had decided it would be her last attempt to make it in the music industry.

Amanda immediately became a favorite on the show. The women loved her – especially the female bikers and activists. She

appealed to them because she refused to change her image and conform to what was popular with the audience and judges. This focus helped propel her to the top eleven in the competition. She said she had fun each week just being herself on the show and not worrying about winning.

Amanda said she is proud of her time on "American Idol." She said the experience put her way ahead of where she would have been otherwise, and it brought her offers that she might never have received without the exposure. I spoke with her not long after the show ended, when she was taking time off to decide what she wanted to do next. At the time she was looking at a potential movie offer and discussing recording opportunities.

Looking back, Amanda said she had no idea how significant an impact she had made until people started approaching her and thanking her for just being herself. Female motorcycle riders and female activists showed up in great numbers to get her autograph and speak to her. Amanda became a role model for women who are comfortable being who they are and not trying to please anyone else. It's pretty cool for a young woman to have that much confidence. And she credits her upbringing and the support of her family and fiancé for allowing her to be "just Amanda."

Learnings:

- Amanda says her decision to try her luck on "American Idol" gave her the opportunity to pursue her music career – an opportunity she wouldn't have had if she hadn't taken the chance.
- Always be yourself and stay true to your convictions.
- No matter what you want to do or change – go for it. It's not the end of the world if it doesn't turn out exactly like you wanted.
- It is better to have tried than to look back when you are older and realize you never took a chance on what you wanted in life.

- Frequently choose to take the road less traveled – we only live once.
- If you have changes you would like to make in life, make them. The only thing that can stop you is…you.

The Courage To Divorce Leads To Happiness

Lesson: *"Sometimes it's ok to be selfish and take care of yourself first. Women tend to be very bad at doing this."*
–Elaine, Business Consultant
North Carolina

Elaine was married at age twenty-two to a man nineteen years her senior. She told me that her father passed away when she was just seventeen, and in hindsight, she feels she was trying to replace him with her husband, Ted.

Elaine fell in love with Ted right away. A friend introduced them on a Friday night, and on Monday Ted showed up with roses at Elaine's workplace. He was everything she had been waiting for: educated with a very good job; a man who took control and made her feel like he was her knight in shining armor.

Elaine and Ted lived together for two years before they were married. Elaine's mother was against the relationship from day one, telling Elaine that Ted was too old and not the right man for her. Elaine's mom was only three years older than Ted. But Elaine introduced Ted to her family and her church anyway, and made him part of her life.

The couple married and moved to California, where Elaine entered the world of the corporate wife. The wife of the CEO of Ted's company liked Elaine instantly and took her under her wing. While Elaine drove a Mercedes and didn't have to work, she was wary of becoming trapped in a life built on material possessions.

She also began to realize that many of the corporate wives were really very unhappy and drank too much. Still, Ted took care of her every need, except one: faithfulness.

One woman was never enough for Ted. On their first anniversary, Elaine prepared a wonderful candlelight dinner and waited for Ted to arrive at 7 p.m. as he had promised. When he was still not home at 10 p.m., Elaine became worried and went to look for him at the corporate apartment from which they had just moved. There she found Ted with another woman. She was so angry that she returned to her car, took a lug wrench from the trunk and shattered the apartment window. Ted and the woman fled, and the police soon arrived.

Elaine said she'll never forget the responding officer and how kind he was to her. When he asked her what had happened, she broke down crying and told him the story. The officer had a necktie pin that said "Jesus Saves," and Elaine saw this as a good sign. The officer told her to leave Ted. He said in all his years, he had learned that Ted's type never changes, and for her future happiness and safety, she should just fly back home to North Carolina. Elaine knew he was right, but she couldn't face her family or her church with the shameful news.

This shame kept Elaine with Ted for more than a decade, and the same scenario played out year after year. He would be unfaithful, and she would forgive him and hope he would change. Ted always handed Elaine the credit card after these episodes, and she could buy extravagant jewelry, clothes or whatever she wanted to make it right. Elaine said she had become swept up in the comfort of being taken care of. She was dependent on Ted and afraid to leave him. She had gotten used to the "good" life.

During the last three years of their marriage, Ted and Elaine maintained separate bedrooms and only made appearances together for the sake of Ted's job. When Ted was transferred to South Carolina, Elaine's prayers were answered. She would be close enough to home to have a support group of friends, and she would work up the courage to be on her own.

At the age of thirty-one, Elaine decided it was time to be true to herself. Not long after the couple's move to South Carolina, Elaine packed her car with all of her possessions and was preparing to go. As she was loading the last items, Ted arrived home early and actually laughed at her when she said she wanted a divorce.

As she drove away, she remembers the sky being so beautiful and clear blue – like a clean slate. She saw this as a sign that she could write what she wanted for herself on that slate, and she did. She got her own little apartment. She got a job and began supporting herself.

A few years later, she met a wonderful man three years her junior. They have been happily married ever since.

Learnings:

- Be true to yourself.
- Sometimes it's ok to be selfish and to take care of yourself first.

Father's Illness Becomes A Wake-Up Call

Lesson: *"Don't be ashamed if everything isn't perfect in your life; we are all human, and it's ok to be human."*

–Hillery Moise, Restaurant Owner
New Orleans

It was a shock for Hillery when she got a call one day telling her that her sixty-two year old father, Mac, had suffered a stroke and was not expected to live. When she and her sister arrived at the

hospital, they joined their mother in the chapel to pray. The doctor entered shortly afterward to tell them he only expected Mac to live another few minutes, and they should prepare.

But the family would not accept that. They continued to pray by his side, and sure enough, Mac survived the night.

They were then told that Mac would never fully recover and never be responsive. Again, the family refused to believe it. Hillery and the family would bring books to Mac and read to him. They would show him pictures of ships and the sea, which were his love and passion. Hillery would bring him stuffed animals to hold. She would put a pen in his hand and help him write the alphabet.

And then one day, Mac started writing the letters on his own. After about six months, he was moved to a rehabilitation facility, where he regained his speech but was still wheelchair-bound. He would joke with the other patients to keep their spirits up.

One night when Hillery and her two sisters were getting dressed to go to a Mardi Gras ball, they received a frantic call from a rehab facility worker who told them that Mac had escaped from the building in his wheelchair. They rushed over and found that their father had wheeled himself out into the parking lot, where he had crashed into a huge oak tree. He was sitting beside the tree laughing. They took him home that night, and he continued to improve until he could walk four miles a day. He lived for another eighteen years.

Her father's experience prompted Hillery to take a look at her own life. She asked herself whether she was really happy, and the answer was no. The reason was her marriage. She had a big house, plenty of money and three lovely children, but she was not in love with her husband, and she was living a lie each day. Everyone thought she had the perfect life, but in reality, she was living according to everyone else's expectations.

During her father's ordeal, Hillery felt that her husband had

not been there for her. In fact, Hillery admitted she had only married him to placate his parents and to keep him from being sent to fight in the Vietnam War. She got married instead of pursuing her own dream of joining the Peace Corps.

One night shortly after her father's illness began, Hillery snapped. Her husband was supposed to pick up a friend at the airport, but he decided at the last minute that she should do it instead. She did as he asked, but after she delivered the guest to their home, she left and checked into a hotel. She ran away for the night to think.

That night she pondered how she had spent most of her life being the perfect daughter, the perfect wife, mother, sister and neighbor, but she had lost herself in the process. And life is short. She needed to be true to herself. She was not happy with her marriage, and that night she decided to do something about it.

She called her husband and told him she needed to talk. She asked him to keep quiet so as not to alert the kids or her family. Instead, he did just the opposite and had the entire family in an uproar by morning. That sealed her decision. She went home, ordered her husband out of the house, and never looked back. She became a single mom with three kids, but she was finally happy. She was being true to herself.

Later she would meet her true love, Ed, who has cared for her children like his own. They are happily married with wonderful grandchildren.

Learnings:

- Don't be ashamed if everything isn't perfect in your life; we are all human, and it's ok to be human.
- Don't live according to the expectations of others.
- Don't try to fix others. You can only fix yourself.

- If you think you have a problem that can't be solved, just wait until tomorrow. Everything looks different after a night's sleep.
- Don't get so caught up in trying to make everything go the way you think it should. Allow things to run their natural course.

Living The Life She Was Meant To

Lesson: *"When you accept yourself as you are, a whole new, wonderful world opens to you."*

–Michelle Toca, Transgender Woman and Retired Law Enforcement Officer Dallas

Michelle was born a man. She lived as Glenn through twenty-one years of marriage and thirty years at the Jefferson Parish Sheriff's Office in metropolitan New Orleans. This transgender woman described to me the many defining moments in her life growing up in the 1950s and 60s. Glenn was raised Catholic, the eldest of four siblings, with an Irish mother and a French father who served in the Marines during World War II.

Michelle told me that she first noticed she was different at about age ten, when she became more interested in hanging out with the girls than with the boys. Her father quickly remedied that by getting Glenn involved in sports. Glenn conformed to the expectations of society at the time, and at age nineteen, he got married. It lasted six months. When Glenn told his wife how he really felt – like a woman trapped in a man's body – she immediately kicked him out of the house and filed for divorce.

At age twenty-one Glenn joined the sheriff's office, beginning what would be a very successful thirty-year career in law enforcement. While responding to a robbery one night, he met a woman named Diane and her two children. He immediately fell in

love, and they were married for twenty-one years. Michelle said that as Glenn, she had the pleasure of not only being in a loving marriage, but of being a father, and now, as Michelle, a grandmother.

Glenn and Diane went through the normal ups and downs of marriage. Glenn had learned to keep his feelings hidden, and as a result, he suffered terrible bouts of depression. Diane was always there to help him through these times, never suspecting that something other than the usual job pressures were to blame. Glenn suppressed his feelings and worked hard to comply with society's rules of how a man is supposed to act. Michelle told me that despite the depression, she would not change a thing about those years.

In 2001, Diane developed cancer. She initially fought it off, but it returned in 2003 to claim her life. It was such a blow to Glenn that he could not work for a month, and he sank into a deep sadness. Michelle said she never would have survived Diane's death had it not been for their wonderfully strong and supportive daughter.

In 2005, Glenn stayed in New Orleans in his capacity as a law enforcement officer during Hurricane Katrina. Michelle described the horrible time spent living out of a squad car and rescuing people from the streets, dodging bullets while struggling to save as many lives as possible.

Glenn's life-transforming moment happened while he was working on the Interstate 10 overpass where storm victims were waiting to be taken out of the city. There were fights over food and water, and a desperate look in people's eyes. At that moment, Glenn realized how brief and fragile life can be. That was the moment he decided to become the person he was meant to be. He never looked back. His decision was made. He was going forward to fully become a woman. A woman named Michelle.

In November 2005, after three decades of dedicated service, Glenn retired from the force to pursue his dream. He spent time

working in gay and transgender bars in the French Quarter, where he would talk with transsexuals about their experience. He asked them questions about their operations and how they felt about the surgery, and about what kind of psychological therapy they had received. He then relocated to Dallas to be close to his daughter. There, he found a good therapist and a doctor to help him begin the process of gender reassignment.

When I interviewed her, Michelle was still about eighteen months away from the full transition. She was taking hormones to give her a more feminine appearance in preparation for her final surgery, and she vowed to return to New Orleans when the operation was complete.

Michelle became a member of a support group of transgender police officers in Dallas. She told me that ninety percent of the people who transition do so later in life. Michelle has attended lectures on the subject and has been inspired by Donna Rose, a national speaker and authority on transgender. Rose wrote a book called *Wrapped in Blue*, which Michelle highly recommends for anyone thinking of making the change.

When I asked Michelle how her new life is different from her old, she was quick to point out a couple of things. She said as a woman, her nurturing point of view and sensitivity have allowed her to see the world differently. As a "rough and ready" cop, she always saw human nature at its worst. But as Michelle, she sees the softer side of life, which she attributes to the female hormones. And when she meets someone for the first time, she is focused on their good qualities instead of being suspicious of the bad.

She said she's also dealing with the fact that women are not treated equally in the world. Having walked in both sets of shoes, she has a unique perspective. When Michelle goes out with a man, she lets him take the lead, although she said that's tough for someone who has been a leader her entire life. I responded that many strong women, myself included, experience difficulties in relationships for the same reason. Sometimes it's hard to find a partner who can accept you as an equal.

Michelle and I also discussed Katrina's impact on the people of New Orleans, and how it has been both a curse and a blessing. As the old saying goes, out of something bad can come something good. For Michelle and many others who lived through it, the storm lifted the veil and exposed what is really important.

Learnings:

- Just do it – whatever it is in your life that you have been waiting to do.
- Be happy with yourself. Don't feel guilty about pursuing your dreams.
- Don't conform to what society or other people expect. Be yourself.
- If you are confident in yourself and respectful of other people, you will receive that in return most of the time.
- Be helpful to others. You can make an impact on others' lives just by taking the time to do something kind.
- Try to really listen and understand people.
- Accept yourself for who you are. Once you do, you can accept others and be happy. It's a wonderful life out there – go find it!

They Go Together…My Divorce And My New Relationship

Lesson: *"Sometimes change is listening to that little voice and realizing when we are supposed to make a change."*
–Kathy Lynn

I had been married for twenty years, and I was content – or

at least thought I was. My husband was wonderful to me – flowers weekly, home-cooked meals. He was my best friend. He had however, been unfaithful to me once at about year twelve of our marriage. At the time, I thought I forgave him. I decided to make a go of the relationship, which I thought was supposed to last forever. I had always been consumed with success and work, so I know I didn't spend enough quality time being what a wife is supposed to be. I guess it was a combination of things that were probably working against us.

The thing is, I thought I was absolutely happy. Then we went on a cruise for our anniversary, and all "hell broke loose," as they say. It was strange how the whole thing unfolded.

My husband was planning a trip to France, where we would cruise down the Seine by barge. But the more I thought about how cold it would be (I just can't do cold weather), I decided we were not going to France in the fall. I wanted a warm vacation and anniversary celebration, but I had no idea where I wanted to go. Well, sometimes fate takes charge – fate or the spiritual guide in our lives. Did it ever happen for me!

That summer I flew to Chicago for the usual, boring corporate meeting. A woman who was also attending walked up to me out of the blue and told me that I had to go on this cruise that she had gone on two months earlier. Her forcefulness took me aback because I barely knew her. But she was insistent. She proceeded to tell me how wonderful it was and that I truly needed to go. So I jotted down the name of the cruise and told her I would look into it when I returned home. I really didn't have any intention of doing so, but again, fate was playing a part here.

When I returned home and started going through my mail, what appears but a brochure about a cruise to the South Pacific! I immediately pulled the name of the cruise I had jotted down in

Chicago. It was the same cruise. The coincidence was too much. I knew I was supposed to go.

Sometimes, making a change is just a matter of listening to that little voice inside telling you, "it's time." I really believe that. So, off my husband and I went four months later to the South Pacific. And wham, bam! Was change ever waiting for me!

On the second night of our cruise, I heard this wonderful piano music coming from one of the entertainment areas on the ship, and I told my husband we should check it out after dinner. When I walked into the piano bar, I immediately made eye contact with the entertainer. Now, I'd never looked at other men during my marriage and never thought of being unfaithful to my husband. I was too busy working and being happy just as I was. However, in the back of my mind, I don't think I ever truly forgave him for cheating on me. In fact, I know I didn't. Anyway, we learned that the entertainer was from New Orleans, my favorite city. The entertainer seemed delighted by the coincidence.

The next morning, I was drawn to the music again, and I found the piano player practicing on a quiet part of the ship. I sat for half an hour and listened as he played classical music, never letting him know I was there. I'm not even sure why I was there myself, but I had to be there. Again, fate was playing a hand. Each day I repeated this routine, sneaking away to listen to him play, and then each night my husband and I would go to the piano bar to see and talk to him. I found myself consumed by him. I hadn't felt this way since I was a teenager, and then never so strongly in my life! I was literally drawn to this stranger in every way – physically, mentally, emotionally – and I had no control over myself. You must understand that I was the master at controlling every aspect of my life, so this really flipped me out! I ended up approaching him one day when he was practicing to tell him how drawn to him I was, and to try and

get it out of my system. Instead, I started a romance that lasted for several years.

Once I made him aware of my feelings, he came to the pool and talked with me that day while my husband slept below deck. Four days later when I departed, I left my phone number and contact information under the piano cover for him to find. He told me later that he knew it would be there. He called me from Tahiti, and we talked by phone and e-mail for two months.

Then, one December day I left the house, telling my family that I was going to a board meeting (which I did attend). Afterward, I flew to Tahiti for a ten-day cruise to be with him and see if what I was feeling was real. I returned home on Christmas Eve and completely changed my life forever. I told my husband that I was leaving him. I couldn't carry on a relationship in secret, so I felt it best to tell him immediately and end it. Within six weeks my husband and I were officially divorced, and I was dating my new friend in New Orleans by Mardi Gras.

Was it fate? Was it middle-age crazy? What the heck was I thinking? Here I was, this conservative, corporate woman who had always done everything as perfectly as I could. I had always played by the rules. What the heck was I doing running off with a piano player? I questioned my decision many times, especially when the relationship was difficult. One day we were madly in love, and the next we couldn't be together without fighting.

We have since parted ways, but we remain good friends. We are so different, and yet we enjoy each other so much. I've had some of the most fun in my life knowing this crazy, spontaneous New Orleans entertainer!

What I know right now for sure is that I trust God to bring the right people into my life, and me into theirs, at just the right time. In January 2009, I began saying a positive affirmation each morning:

"The love of a perfect partner for me will come into my life."

Life is good, and God does answer prayers and positive affirmations. I'm waiting to see who shows up next!

Learnings:

- Don't react too quickly. Give yourself time to make sure what you are feeling is the real thing.
- On the flip side, don't be afraid to change if it is the real thing. I believe my husband and I were meant to be together for those years we shared, and I still love him. He is one of my best friends, but we had to go through the messy and nasty divorce stuff that most people go through in order to get here. My piano entertainer was meant to come into my life at that time to help me on to the next part of my journey. We were together six years, but it was not a bed of roses.
- Have your finances in order, and always make sure you know what your financial status is, man or woman. One person should not handle all of the finances in a marriage. Be informed.
- Draw up a prenuptial agreement if you need one. Get divorced in the right state! Know the laws.
- Try to work things out as much as you can, and use the same attorney if you can to save money and feelings.
- Marriage is not for everyone.
- Be happy and live the life you are meant to live. Sometimes you have to make the tough choices.
- I truly believe that people come and go in our lives exactly when they are meant to. There is a bigger plan for each of us...we just have to be open to it.
- I think some people are actually happier being single and surrounding themselves with friends, family and special romances.
- If you fall in love...go for it. You only live once.

Lesson 2 Questions

Where in your life do you need to make a change that you have been avoiding or have been afraid to make?

What would making that change do to your life?

What steps can you take to make that change?

LESSON 3

NEVER TAKE LIFE FOR GRANTED; PUT FAMILY AND GOD FIRST

"The whole of life is but a moment of time. It is our duty, therefore, to use it, not to misuse it."

Plutarch

A Brain Tumor Changes Her Life Forever

Lesson: *"Health is so important to living your life to the fullest. You need to be the best you can be physically and mentally."*
–Olivia Foret, Radiology Student
Louisiana

When talking with Olivia, you feel you are talking to a much older soul – older, and with a certain maturity that most young people don't possess.

Maybe it's because of everything she has been through. She is a confident, committed woman with high expectations of herself, but she has also had her share of looking at her life and wondering, "Am I ok?"

When she was nineteen, Olivia went to visit her boyfriend in Shreveport, Louisiana, about a five-hour drive from her home. After arriving, she became violently ill with a migraine. She passed it off as just a bug and spent the entire weekend resting.

On Monday, she got up early to head back home, but after driving for a while she saw a "Welcome to Texas" sign and became confused. How could she be in Texas when she was driving home to South Louisiana? After pulling off the road and crying, she finally settled down and returned to her boyfriend's house. She realized that something was very wrong. She called her mother, who helped her get back home the following day and scheduled an appointment with a neurologist.

After two MRIs, doctors found a tumor on Olivia's pituitary gland. They told her it could cause blindness if not addressed immediately. They assured her that it was not life-threatening, and that she would be just fine. But at such a young age, it was the last thing she expected. Olivia was really, truly scared for the first time in her life.

The surgery was scheduled for July 15, two days before Olivia's twentieth birthday. Complications arose, and she ended up staying in intensive care for five days. It was there that she said she had the best birthday of her life.

She said it was the best because everyone who really cared for her was there. The nurses and the doctors were wonderful. All of her friends and family came to the hospital to show her how much they loved her. And it was through this experience that she learned who her true friends were. Some of the people she thought were her best friends, including her boyfriend, didn't even show up, while others she thought were just acquaintances came with gifts.

One year after the successful surgery, a friend told Olivia about a competition called the Body for LIFE Challenge. She told Olivia she should consider entering the competition. It would only last three months, and people had amazing results.

Olivia and her friend bought the Body for LIFE book and talked with others about participating as a team. Five of them entered the competition, and Olivia and her friend finished it together. It was a tough commitment – Olivia had to change her eating and drinking habits, start a gym routine and maintain sharp mental focus the entire time. At the end of the three months, she had transformed herself by losing pounds and inches and developing a mental stamina that serves her to this day.

Learnings:

- When you go through tough times in your life, you learn who your real friends are.
- Olivia said when she experiences hard times, she turns to God for strength. She said her faith in God can see her through anything.
- Self-worth comes from being proud of who you are. Be proud of yourself and your body no matter what size you are or shape you are in. Carve out the time to take care of yourself.

- Only by taking care of yourself can you be at your best for those you love.
- Health is vital for living your life to the fullest. You need to be the best you can be physically and mentally.
- Honesty and self-worth are crucial to happiness. All else will follow if you put God first and your family second, and be honest and take care of yourself.

The Loss Of A Brother

Lesson: *"To reach out to others in your grief is the best remedy…seek help from others who are going through the same loss as you."*
–Carolina Gallop, Fashion Designer and Event Planner
New Orleans

Carolina was born in Honduras to a large, loving family. She moved to Boston with her mother and several of her eight siblings when she was nine years old. She later moved to California for a short stay, and then came to New Orleans, where she fell in love with the city and made it her permanent home.

She relayed to me one of the most difficult life changes she has ever experienced: the loss of her brother when he was just twenty-five years old.

"Burying your siblings is tough, and something I never thought about," she said. "I guess we just go through life, get up and go to work, enjoying what we do, thinking the ones we love will always be there."

Carolina's brother was shot by a sniper as he sat in a Boston park with his friends after school. She said the pain of his death was made worse by the violent way in which he died.

"I had a very difficult time," Carolina said. "I tried to throw myself into his casket at the funeral, just to give you an idea of how

upset and emotional I was over the loss. I went through the stages of grieving with my family, and I stayed with them in Boston for three months after his death. Then, when I came back to New Orleans, I went into a cocoon and didn't keep in touch with my family or friends at all. I now realize that I was trying to keep from being hurt so badly again by pushing everyone I loved away."

Carolina moved to Florida after Katrina and began attending a class at a local college. One day, the professor asked everyone to share a personal experience with death. As everyone told their stories, they cried.

"I didn't volunteer to tell my story until the teacher called on me, and boy am I glad she did," Carolina said. "I chose to talk about my brother, and afterward I realized I was distancing myself from my family because of my fear of losing one of them again and not wanting to go through that pain. That day in class was a turning point for me with my grief."

Carolina said she now stays in close contact with her family and travels to Honduras and Boston to see them as often as she can.

Learnings:

- Carolina said she has learned how important it is to spend quality time with her family. She said she had been busy living life, and assumed that her siblings would always be there. After losing her brother, she realized she had neglected that relationship. She now takes time to visit her siblings frequently. The loss of her brother brought her closer to the rest of her family, and also to her husband.
- Never take life for granted.
- Reaching out to others in times of grief is the best remedy, especially when you connect with those who have experienced similar loss.

Cancer Fighter For Life

Lesson: *"Yesterday is over, live for today," and "It is what it is."*

–Cathy Gaudet, Mother, Wife, Administrator
New Orleans

Cathy told me that cancer has caused the most significant changes in her life. That's *changes* – not change. Cancer has made an impact more than once.

Cathy's mother was diagnosed with breast cancer in 1971 at the age of thirty-seven. Cathy was one of five children ranging in age from nine to sixteen. Her parents chose not to tell the children how bad the prognosis was. By the time Cathy's mother was diagnosed, the cancer had spread too far and she would not be able to beat it. Still, she chose to undergo what was then a new form of treatment called chemotherapy.

Cathy can remember her mother losing her hair, throwing up often and having a table full of pills next to her bed. She also remembers seeing the scar on her mother's chest after her mastectomy, and the breast prostheses that she would fit into her bra when she went out in public.

Her mother lost her battle on May 25, 1972. As the eldest daughter, Cathy assumed the role of woman of the house at the age of twelve.

Cathy's aunt survived both breast and ovarian cancer. Cathy said she has been a tremendous source of strength for her through the years.

In December 1990, Cathy's nephew was diagnosed with Wilms' tumor, a kidney cancer that mostly affects children. She said it was difficult to watch the seven-month-old undergo surgery, chemotherapy and radiation.

"But I am happy to say that today my nephew is a happy, healthy teenager who is currently president of his senior class and a member of his school basketball team," she said.

Cathy started routine mammograms at the age of thirty-five. She and her sister both had lumpectomies that revealed pre-cancerous cells in her sister and a benign cyst in Cathy. Cathy thought it was only a matter of time before she would be diagnosed, but the disease found a way to surprise her once again.

"In May of 2006 while out of town at a training class, I received a phone call from my son telling me that my husband, Rooky, was acting very different," she said. "I called Rooky to talk to him, and he assured me that it was just a sinus headache and he would take some medicine and sleep it off.

"I asked my son to take my husband to a clinic to see if they could diagnose his problem. My son called me back and said that the clinic doctor had given my husband a prescription and suggested we schedule an MRI sometime the following week. My sister-in-law insisted we get a second opinion, and she scheduled a visit with her doctor the following morning.

"I made arrangements to fly home that morning. When my brother picked me up at the airport, he told me that Rooky had a mass in his brain. I got to the emergency room just in time to see the neurologist. He informed us that the mass needed to be removed as soon as possible, and he put my husband on steroids to reduce swelling in the brain so that the surgery could be performed. My husband was diagnosed on Friday and had brain surgery the following Monday. The weekend was a blur.

"The surgery confirmed the worst. Rooky had GBM grade IV, the worst form of brain cancer there is. He was put into ICU and we were told that we needed to watch his left side for movement.

The brain surgery had caused a stroke that affected the left side of his body. We were told that he would probably be wheelchair-bound for life and would probably not make it to Christmas 2006."

Cathy said as Rooky was being transferred from his ICU bed to his bed on the oncology unit, he called her over to his side.

"I just saw Fr. Francis Seelos, Blessed Virgin Mary and Jesus Christ," he said. "Just like that: boom, boom, boom."

Cathy said she knew at that moment that God was telling them that they would be alright. Her husband was released from the hospital thirty-nine days later.

Cathy said her husband has always had a positive attitude. His incredible faith, will and desire to live have inspired her tremendously. Her husband always says, "Yesterday is over – live for today," and "It is what it is." Those sayings have kept her going.

Cathy said her family has learned that life is based on choices.

"When faced with a devastating time in our lives such as a diagnosis of cancer, we had choices to make," she said. "We could both sit there and feel sorry for ourselves, or we could do like the Tim McGraw song says: 'Live Like You Were Dying.'"

During the period in 2006 and 2007 when her husband was ill, Cathy was extremely busy. She continued to work full-time, she took Rooky to therapy three days a week, and she cared for him at home. Cathy scheduled her own yearly check-up and intended to get a mammogram, but she just didn't have time to take care of it right away.

When she finally did have her mammogram, she received a phone call the next day from a technician asking her to come in for a closer look at her right breast. Cathy underwent an ultrasound, and then a biopsy, and was diagnosed with breast cancer.

Cathy told me she always thought that she'd be diagnosed eventually, but now? In the middle of her husband's illness? She then admitted that one night during prayer she put her hand on her husband's head and told God that if he would give her a little bit of Rooky's illness so that he could be here longer, she'd take it.

Needless to say, Cathy moved very quickly. Soon after her diagnosis, she underwent a double mastectomy and breast reconstruction. Her husband was on her mind constantly, and she knew the sooner she took care of herself, the sooner she'd be able to care for him again.

Cathy said she and Rooky learned the meaning of "in sickness and in health" when, on Dec. 14, 2007, their twenty-eighth wedding anniversary, they sat side-by-side in the hospital's outpatient oncology room and received their chemotherapy together. They had lost their hair together, learned how to treat their chemotherapy side effects together and leaned on each other for strength.

"It can only beat you if you let it," Cathy said. "We have learned to try to stay positive. I read somewhere that for every minute you waste worrying about what might happen, you lose a minute of happiness.

"Rooky says it is what it is, so we pick up the cards and move forward. We have learned to live. We don't put off until tomorrow anything we can do today. We have learned that the things that used to seem so important are so unimportant. Having the support of our children and family is what matters most. I personally could not have made it through this last year without the support of my family. They have been my rock."

Learnings

- Live for today. We are not promised tomorrow.

- Make a list of the things you want to do before you die and do it!
- Family and friendships are most important in life.
- Trust that God has a plan.

A Retreat Changes Her Life

Lesson: *"We must take time for ourselves in order to be the best we can be in life."*

–Lily, Retired Insurance Executive
Chicago

Lily never realized her life would change as much as it did when she attended a leadership retreat based on the book *The 7 Habits of Highly Successful People* by Stephen Covey.

Lily found herself at a former Catholic retreat center in a room with only a twin bed. There was no phone, radio, TV or any type of communication. Each night she was given an assignment to examine a different part of her life.

It was a life-changing experience for Lily. One night, the assignment was to make a list of the five most important things to her, and another list of what she spent her time on each day.

The next day the instructor spoke about how people find themselves physically and mentally stressed when the two lists don't match. We may not even be aware of the stress, but it wears us down little by little over the years. Lily realized that eighty percent of her day was spent on things that were nowhere near her top five.

The next night she decided to redesign how she spent her time. She decided to retire at age fifty-five instead of waiting until she was sixty-six.

When she returned home after the retreat, Lily shifted her focus to her top five priorities. She had wonderful results in her

personal life and was more satisfied with her job than she had been in years. No longer did she bring problems home to her family. When she left work after ten hours each day, she devoted her time at home to what she felt was most important, including her family and friends. She also changed departments at work and was much happier in the last eight years of her career.

A simple three-day retreat had changed her life both personally and professionally.

Learning:

- In order to think, we must take time for ourselves with no interruptions. At the retreat, Lily learned to make this a part of her daily life. Now, for half an hour each morning, she spends time reflecting on God and reading spiritual works. She said this gets her focused and centered for the day.

Losing Her Brother To Cancer Changes Her Life Forever

Lesson:

"Feel the fear and do it anyway."
–Pam Irvin, Mother, Wife, Business Owner
Atlanta

Until she was thirty-seven years old, Pam was a person who never made any real changes in her life. The cancer death of her younger brother, Tony, altered that. His death made her look at life very differently. Pam used to think she needed material things to be happy, but she has since discovered that material possessions don't really matter to her at all. Her brother's death taught her that family, friends and the love she feels for them are the most important things.

A year or so after losing her brother, Pam took a month off

work to travel throughout India. When she returned, she quit the job she had held for fifteen years at IBM. These major changes made it easier for her to make other, smaller changes in her life. Pam told me that change can be difficult, depending upon your attitude. She said it took everything she had to make her career change, and she just kept telling herself that she would be ok no matter what happened.

Two months after leaving IBM, Pam attended a life-change program at the Hippocrates Institute in Florida. A month after that, she met a man from Italy in an Atlanta grocery store, of all places. They started talking, and he asked her to go out with him that evening.

"We don't do things like that in the U.S., going out alone with a perfect stranger!" she told him.

But she ended up doing it anyway.

Three days later, the man returned home to Rome. For six months they wrote to each other and talked on the phone, and then Pam went to Italy for a two-week visit. She didn't return home until two months later, and then it was only to sell her house and prepare for marriage and a new life in Italy.

The couple wanted children and ended up adopting a boy and girl from Orissa, India. It took three trips to India in 10 months to make it happen, but they did it.

Today, Pam has a wonderful man in her life and two beautiful children. Pam has lots of love, and she knows very clearly what is important.

Learnings:

- The things that helped her through her career change were daily yoga, meditation and reading self-help books. Her favorite book was *You Can Heal Your Life* by Louise Hay. Pam also met with a counselor to talk about her fear. The talks led her to the realization that her fear of change was irrational. Change is a constant in the universe.

- Pam feels there are specific lessons that each person's life reveals. She said we are guided to these lessons, but it's up to us to have the courage to accept and learn them. Self-awareness – knowing who you are and being at peace with that knowledge – makes the journey easier. Some say that only five percent of us will ever achieve such a level of self-awareness. Pam's advice to others? Feel the fear and do it anyway!

Losing The Most Important Person In My Life

Lesson: *"Even if you think you spend enough time with someone you love, spend more time while you can. Enjoy them every moment of every day that God allows."*
–Kathy Lynn

My mother… She was always there for me.

Whether I was happy, sad or celebrating some grand or small accomplishment, it was always more important to her than it was to me, or at least that's how she made me feel. She was my confidante. Each night at 7 p.m., we talked on the phone about the day's events or just about life in general. I used to imagine having her with me well into old age, and all the things we would do together once I retired. Instead, I lost her to lung cancer when she was just sixty-nine years old. I still sometimes look at the clock at 7 p.m. and wait for her call. I used to call her cell phone just to hear her voice, and when I would hear the automated message saying she's not available, I would cry.

My mother was and always will be the most important person in my life. I was blessed to have been born into such a loving, caring family. My mother's parents were just like her. Everyone loved them, and their home was the gathering place. Even their pastor visited each weekend for Sunday dinner.

From my earliest memories of school, my mother was always

the homeroom mother, and the kids loved her. She just had a way with people. Complete strangers would stop and talk with her in the grocery store, bank, or wherever she was. She was a people magnet and she loved to listen to their stories. I realize now that this was her purpose in life – to be a friend to everyone, and to be there for others.

Many of my friends and former boyfriends adopted her as their second mother, and she was there for them when they needed her. Recently, an old friend whom I hadn't spoken to in more than twenty years called to tell me how much my mother influenced her. She said my mother had been a role model, influencing her in her own role as a mother.

We almost lost my mother at age sixty-six to an undiagnosed problem with her pancreas. The doctors told us that her body was shutting down and she wouldn't last the night, but we knew it wasn't her time. And so we prayed. I had friends all across the country praying for her, and she pulled through. The doctors called her a miracle. She was in and out of ICU for the next six months before she was able to come home to us. I was with her the entire time. While she was hospitalized, doctors discovered her lung cancer. Once she was stabilized, the doctors performed surgery and gave her a good prognosis.

I bought her a little book called *Reflections from a Mother's Heart*, which asked her questions about her life. She was supposed to complete the book for the family to enjoy one day when she wasn't around anymore. For the next two years I tried my best to get her to complete the book, but she wouldn't do it. It sat by her bed, empty and unread. Finally, I quit asking her, thinking she would do it when she was ready.

We enjoyed her for three more years before the cancer came

back with a vengeance, spreading to her liver. The chemotherapy wasn't working, and she died suddenly one night from a heart attack. That was exactly how she wanted to go. She wanted it to be quick with no pain and suffering, and she got her wish.

The day after her funeral service, I went to her bedroom to try and find something for my sister, and I saw the book I had given her next to the bed. I looked at it longingly, wishing she had completed it and feeling sad that she hadn't. I returned to the bedroom later that day to look through some of her items and just feel close to her. After a few moments, I was drawn to the book once again, and I picked it up. When I opened it, I saw her handwriting inside. She had completed it for me after all. I cried tears of joy. I think it was her way of comforting me that very day when I needed her. She knew I would find it, and she would once again be there for me.

Describing what it's like to lose a loved one is difficult. Losing someone you love that much is so painful, mentally and physically. I was basically in shock for the first month. I moved forward and took care of arrangements for the two services we had, one in Texas and one in Virginia. But it wasn't until later that I really came to grips with what had happened. I realized that there would be no more phone calls and no more birthday wishes. It left a great emptiness in my soul.

I don't think we ever really get over losing a loved one. We learn to move forward and remember the wonderful times, but I don't think we ever really *get over* it. I was blessed to have two wonderful friends who kept me busy and involved the year after I lost my mom. They have become my adopted mom and the older sister I never had.

I only wish that I had been able to spend more time with my mother and talk to her about death and how she felt about it. Now,

all I have left are wonderful memories and the fact that she made me the person that I am today. I will continue to live my life to the fullest, being the best I can be in honor and celebration of her.

Learnings:

- At the toughest times in our lives, friends and community are so important in helping us deal with our grief.
- Even if you think you spend enough time with someone you love, spend more time while you can. Enjoy them every day, every moment that God allows. Tell them you love them every day. You can never tell someone enough how important they are.
- Talk to loved ones about death. Don't feel awkward – it's part of life.
- You need friends to get through the tough times. Lean on them, and give back to them when they need you.
- Don't just trust what the doctors say. Look for alternative treatments and learn from others about what has worked for them.

Lesson 3 Questions

How much quality time do you spend with the people you care most about?

If it is not enough, what can you change in your life to make more time for them?

LESSON 4

THERE IS SOMETHING IN THIS WORLD GREATER THAN YOU

"Man is what he believes."

Anton Chekhov

A Meeting With Martin Luther King Jr. Reveals Her Calling

Lesson:

"There has to be something in your life that you are willing to die for."
–Yvonne Sharpe, Retired Fortune 100 Executive
Chicago

Yvonne was a black teenager growing up in the South in the late 1950s at a time of tremendous social and cultural change. She describes herself as very fortunate to have had parents who were teachers, and who exposed her and her brother to all facets of life.

Yvonne's parents would take her and her brother on road trips to New York and Chicago to let them see how African-Americans lived in other parts of the country. As a rule, the family would pack their food and drive nonstop until they were above Maryland – a safe distance from the South. Yvonne said she was taught as a young girl not to make eye contact with or speak to a white person unless they spoke to her first.

Yvonne's father was someone who was firm in his principles. He would always say: "There has to be something in your life that you are willing to die for in order for your life to have meaning or purpose."

One evening, Yvonne's father told her that he was taking her to church, where a training session would expose her to a concept that would change the world. He said she didn't have to participate, but he wanted her to hear the lesson. The speaker at the session that night was a man named Martin Luther King Jr.

As Dr. King spoke about civil rights and nonviolence, Yvonne became so inspired that she signed up to be trained to walk in marches for social equality. She figured that if black people paid taxes, they should be able to drink out of the same water fountains

and use the same bathrooms as white people, and be allowed to move about freely in the parks and other facilities that their money supported.

That night Yvonne was trained in the ways of peaceful protest. The marchers-in-training practiced protective moves to be used in case dogs or water hoses were turned on them. It became her calling.

"I believe God was saying it was time for me to take a stand for my people and the generations to come," she said. "And if I had to die to do it, so be it."

That call came several years later during Yvonne's senior year in high school in Elizabeth City, North Carolina. She was told she would be leading fifty marchers to a peaceful sit-in at a local drug store with a fountain shop. They walked in two-by-two formation down the street, passing dogs and water hoses along the way.

When the marchers arrived at the drugstore with Yvonne out in front, they were met by the owner's shotgun-wielding wife. She pointed the gun at Yvonne's face and dared the group to cross the threshold of the shop. At that moment, Yvonne remembered her father's words: "There has to be something in your life that you are willing to die for in order for your life to have meaning or purpose." Yvonne knew that even if she died, others would have a better life, and the world would be a better place.

But before the marchers could cross the threshold, police descended on them, handcuffed everyone and took them to jail. All fifty spent the night standing shoulder-to-shoulder in a cell meant for two to four people. When Yvonne craned her neck to look out the cell window, she saw her father's car parked outside the jail. A sense of calm came over her. She knew that he had his shotgun and was risking his life to protect those inside.

The next day, all of the marchers were found guilty. Those

from the local community received three years of probation. Outsiders, or "troublemakers" as they were called, were sent to the chain gang for six months.

We all know the rest of the story. The civil rights movement swept the United States, and the brave actions of Yvonne and others like her are now a permanent part of history. They did indeed change the world.

Learnings:

- There is something in the world greater than you. The earlier we learn it, the better off we are.
- People are happiest when they focus on the bigger world outside of themselves.
- Learn to ask yourself: "What do you want your gravestone to say about your life?" This will give you a sharp focus on what you do each and every day.
- Learn to judge people as individuals instead of grouping them in categories.

Hurricane Katrina Changes His Life Forever

Lesson: *"The most important thing in life is helping others. If you don't expect anything in return for helping others and you get something anyway, it is a double blessing."*
–Vinnie Pervel, Business Owner,
Renovator of Historic Homes
New Orleans

They were a determined group. Vinnie and his partner Gregg, Vinnie's elderly mother, and a neighbor named Gareth all stayed in New Orleans during Hurricane Katrina to protect their homes, their belongings and their neighborhood. Vinnie and Gareth slept on the porch each night to guard the house, while his mother and Gregg

slept in the bedrooms upstairs. Vinnie said the group always had dinner at dusk, before "the vampires" came out.

By vampires he was referring to the people who would come out after dark to loot and exchange gunfire. Vinnie would cut off his generator and lights because he was afraid the vampires would steal them.

As the storm moved ashore overnight Sunday and Monday morning, the electricity failed. Vinnie said he knew by Thursday night that he was experiencing something that would change him forever.

"How dark it was that Thursday night," he remembered. "There were no stars or moon. I remember Gareth said, 'Vinnie, Katrina even stole the moon.' It was a hot 98 degrees with no wind, and the city was in complete darkness. The only thing we could see were the three gas lanterns in front of our house. All you could hear was gunfire in the distance, and once in a while, close by.

"I told Gareth, 'This is what the battle of New Orleans must have been like when people thought the city was going to be burned down.' With no communications, it was like going back in time."

That morning at about 4:30, Vinnie and Gareth began to fall asleep when they were jolted awake by what sounded like a barrage of gunfire all around them.

"I remember Gareth saying, 'Vinnie, they are burning us out,'" Vinnie said. "All we could see was smoke and flames. Then mom yelled, 'They are coming through the window!'"

The group ran to the back of the house to try to find the source of the flames, and then realized that what they were seeing and hearing was a warehouse exploding on the other side of the Mississippi River. The force of the blast seemed to shake the entire city.

After Thursday, the neighbors who lived behind Vinnie told him they were leaving the city. That left the back of Vinnie's home exposed and unprotected, which terrified him. So he propped up two ladders on the back fence as an escape. It was like being in a war. He knew if the vampires came, they would come to the front of the house. So they closed the shutters and stayed on the top porch at night. They had it all planned out.

Vinnie's mom told him she didn't think she'd be able to climb the ladders fast enough to get away if they were attacked. Vinnie reassured her that he would help get her over. They all went to bed that night not knowing if they would be dead or alive the next morning.

Vinnie knew something had to change. He said he realized he had to quit thinking of himself and put the others first, especially his mom. In a desperate and heart-wrenching moment, he decided that if they were attacked, he would shoot his mother first, and then Gregg next to prevent them from suffering.

The next night he told Gareth his plan.

"Buddy, it's you and me," Vinnie said. "Whoever shoots first, the other fool is just left."

Now, that sounds extreme in this day and time in the United States, but it's a testament to how mentally fragile the people of New Orleans were. With little sleep and no outside communication, they had no idea what was going on in the world or even just across the river. They were afraid for their lives that first week. It was an out-of-control time.

Vinnie knew his family would never be the same again. There was no one to help them – no government agency, police or fire department.

"There was no one you could really count on," he said.

Of all the people to think about at such a time, Vinnie said it

was Rush Limbaugh and Charlton Heston who came to mind. First, he said Rush's constant lectures on how people shouldn't rely on the government came back to him over and over again as he sat on that porch protecting his family and home. It would be ten days before they saw a police car and two weeks before the National Guard came to town. They were truly on their own.

Second, Vinnie had started getting gun magazines about three years before the storm, and he didn't fully understand why. He initially thought he had joined the National Republican Association, but later realized he had joined the National Rifle Association, which had Charlton Heston as a spokesperson at the time. As he sat in the post-storm chaos, Vinnie was thankful it was the NRA he had joined. He now fully realized how important his gun was for protection.

For the next few weeks the group remained without power, and that meant no TV, no radio. They used a generator for light, and their landline telephone worked sporadically. People could call in, but Vinnie and the family could not call out. No cell phones worked. So the group established a daily routine to try to develop a sense of normalcy. Vinnie would check on the older people in the neighborhood and the pets that were left behind. He fed people when he could and rescued animals. His mom manned the phone and took messages.

One evening, a woman who used to live in the neighborhood called them from Houston. They knew her by her e-mail name: Pollymom. Pollymom would call every night, and she became their link to the outside world. She set up a blog and helped them communicate with neighbors that had scattered across the United States. It felt like things were getting a little better.

Then, it happened.

On the second Tuesday after the storm, Vinnie was attacked. He was on his way to a neighbor's home to turn off the power, and he had just gotten out of his van when he saw a car pull up behind him. Two men got out of the car and approached Vinnie, asking for directions out of the neighborhood. One of the men had a large stick in his pocket. After giving them directions, Vinnie turned to go and the man struck him in the head. Vinnie fell, his head hitting a brick planter on the way down. The vampires turned him over, searching for the keys to his van. Vinnie remembers trying to get up and chase them, but he couldn't. The pain was too intense. About a month later when medical care was available, Vinnie discovered that he had suffered a massive concussion.

Days after the attack, the military finally arrived to announce a mandatory evacuation. Even though the residents had survived Katrina and the looting and chaos that followed, they were being told to leave. Vinnie would not have it, and in the end, the people were allowed to stay and continue to assist the neighborhood. As it turned out, Vinnie's neighborhood was among the first to start functioning again after the storm.

Gareth and Vinnie also took care of an eighty-two year old woman who had returned to the neighborhood from a nursing home. She was legally blind, and her family was still out of town, so Vinnie and Gareth began delivering food to her daily. One day Vinnie heard dogs barking in the home next door. Each day that he visited the woman, he noticed the barking becoming weaker and weaker. Finally, he couldn't take it any longer. He went to the home and kicked in the back door, and a pit bull puppy and an old dog with three legs came hopping out. They were so happy to see him, and Vinnie added them to his daily rounds.

Not long afterward, Vinnie came face-to-face with the dogs' owners. He walked in one day to find a man, woman and two children being interviewed by a local reporter. They asked Vinnie if he was the one who had been feeding the dogs. When he said yes,

the woman ran to him and kissed him. The children thanked him. The man started to cry.

"That was all the thanks I needed," Vinnie said.

In another instance, Vinnie replaced dormers that had blown off of an elderly neighbor's home. When the homeowner returned and found out what he had done, she gave him a thank-you card with ten $100 bills inside. This was a senior citizen living on fixed income. Vinnie gave it back to her, but he said he will never forget how it made him feel.

Vinnie said helping others and being there for his neighbors is what allowed him to survive the experience. It kept him focused. Curiously, he said the hardest part was accepting thanks. He received a plaque from his neighborhood association. People brought him steaks, wine baskets, water and gas to thank him and his family for rescuing their pets or protecting their property. The gifts just kept coming as people returned home. Vinnie said seeing the thankful eyes of his neighbors made it all worthwhile. Vinnie's service had been his lifeline. By helping others, he saved himself.

Learnings:

- It's ok to accept things from people without feeling embarrassed.
- The most important thing in life is helping others.
- If you expect something in return for doing good, you will be disappointed.
- If you don't expect anything in return for helping others, and you get something anyway, it is a double blessing.

My Father Taught Me The Most Important Life Lessons

Lesson: *"People are the most important thing in life."*

–Ken Graham, Ph.D., Business Consultant
Chicago

Ken told me that his father didn't live very long, but in the time he had him, he taught Ken important lessons about life. His dad taught him how to deal with people and gave him a passion for adventure.

When Ken was twelve, his father told him they were going to a picnic. When Ken became very excited, his father told him they were only staying for a little while. He said that if Ken was with him, it would be easier for him to leave early, and he wouldn't be expected to drink alcohol or stay and play cards.

"My father was the No. 2 man at a steel mill in the Northeast," Ken said. "When we went to the picnic I was too young to understand people's reaction to my father, but I understood that they treated him differently as we walked from table to table to greet everyone."

A few years later, a recession hit and the mill had to lay off about half of its workforce. Ken's family had a large house that was in need of fixing up, so his father hired three of the men who had been laid off to do the work. A contract was drawn up, and it was strictly business. The men worked for several weeks at the house, and during that time Ken and his brother got to know them.

"Each day when they would clean up, they would use the water hose to wash things down," Ken said. "If we happened to be around, they would spray us with the hose. We acted like the silly adolescents we were, playing around and roughhousing."

One day, Ken's dad came home from work when they were in the middle of one of their afternoon water fights. He quickly told

all of them to be careful and make sure no one got hurt. The men immediately stopped, but Ken and his brother were upset that their fun had been taken away. At that point Ken said the men told him and his brother something that has stayed with them for life.

They explained that Ken's father was a very special man to them and to the other workers at the mill. By telling them to be careful, he was being responsible. He was taking care of them like he took care of people at the mill every day, making sure they were safe. They told Ken that his father did this not only because it was his job, but because he genuinely cared about people. They went on to say that the mill workers were required to put in eight hours of work, even on slow days. While other managers would assign menial tasks just to pass the time, Ken's dad would tell them to go home to their families when they finished the job. They knew he cared about them, and they respected him greatly. He was a hero at the mill.

Ken said his father taught him other lessons through travel.

"We would get in the car each summer and spend three or four weeks driving and exploring new places," Ken said. "Sometimes we would drive across the entire country. When we would stop for meals, my dad always chose roadside diners.

"When the waitress would approach, my father would call her by name if she was wearing a name tag and ask her questions, like: 'Betty, are you having a good day?' and, 'What is important for us to see while we are in your town?' In doing this, he made Betty feel like a person, not just a waitress.

Ken said in watching his father interact with others, he learned to appreciate that each person and what they do is important. He now understands that his father wanted his sons to experience life with different types of people at every level and to understand how important each person is to the whole.

The lessons paid off for Ken when he was traveling in Mexico with a business partner who spoke fluent Spanish. Ken, on the other hand, had just one year of Spanish under his belt. One morning, they had an appointment with the CEO of a large company.

"As we drove to the appointment, my partner prepped me on protocol," Ken said. "She explained that if the CEO greeted us in English, it was ok to conduct the meeting in English. But if he greeted us in Spanish, we would have to do business in Spanish, and I would just have to keep up as best as I could."

As they entered the CEO's office, Ken's partner had to take an emergency phone call and stepped out. As she did, the CEO came up and greeted Ken in Spanish.

"I remembered my dad's lessons and just went for it," Ken said. "I apologized for my poor Spanish, but said I would try to converse with him. We talked for about fifteen minutes before my partner joined us. At the end of the session, the CEO pulled out a little Mexican flag and presented it to me. We got the account. He later told my partner that he was impressed by someone who spoke so little Spanish but was brave and polite enough to try."

Learnings:

- Whatever you do in life, make sure to put people first.
- Everyone has an important role to play in life. It's how we treat each other in these roles that makes the difference.

85 Years Young, And Living Life To The Fullest Each Day

Lesson: *"CNN becomes many people's best friend after age sixty, and that is one of the reasons they get old."*

–Ms. Irene Burrus, Retiree and Volunteer
New Orleans

"Eighty-five years young" is so appropriate when describing this outgoing, high-energy lady affectionately known as Ms. Irene. She has made such a positive impact on her community over the past forty years. From working in the tourism bureau to help her city put its best face forward, to being one of the most active volunteers in New Orleans, she is blessed to be just as sharp and active as she was at age thirty. In fact, she was awarded one of the state's highest honors for nonprofit volunteers: the Louisiana Heroine Award.

When I asked her about growing up and about her great zest for life and her ability to stay so young at heart, she told me about living through the Great Depression and about her mother's death.

Ms. Irene was seven years old when the Depression hit. She said most people didn't have much in the way of material things, and even though she was very young, she vividly remembers many people committing suicide when they felt they had lost everything and gave up hope. She remembers how sad it was to see people who thought they had nothing to live for. She vowed then to live her own life to the fullest.

Years later, when Ms. Irene was thirteen, her mother died. Before she passed away, she gathered her five children around her and made them make some very important promises: that they would do the best they could, that they would stay together and take care of each other, and that they would do the right things in life.

Ms. Irene said that one of the biggest times of change in her life came between the ages of sixty and eighty, when she realized that she was not going to change the world, but she could work within it to help others. She said it's important for people at that age to find their niche, and she stressed the importance of keeping busy after retirement.

"CNN becomes many people's best friend after age sixty, and that is one of the reasons they get old." she said.

Maintaining a connection to others and staying active were recurring themes in Ms. Irene's stories and thoughts on aging successfully. She mentioned a study about a group of people who live in a remote, mountainous region of Russia. She said they live unusually long lives and are very independent because they're cut off from most of civilization. They have to take care of themselves and each other. Ms. Irene said that she thinks this is the difference between people who go to a nursing home and give up their independence and people who are able to remain on their own. She said the former don't live long lives because they have lost their independence and reason for living. Ms. Irene firmly believes that seniors need to think for themselves and make their own decisions, pay their own bills each month, and stay active and involved.

Learnings:

- Do everything in moderation: eating, drinking, TV, exercise, gambling. Don't let anything become an addiction.
- Have friends of all ages, and make sure they are diverse in every way. You learn more from people who are different from you.
- Be part of many different clubs and organizations that have diverse memberships.
- Choose a life partner whom you respect and who will give you your space to do what you want in life.
- Stay informed. Read newspapers and magazines, listen to smart people and learn from them, and watch educational shows on TV to keep your mind active.
- Don't turn your business affairs over to someone else. The more involved you are and the more responsibility you maintain, the better your mental health.
- Have enthusiasm for life.
- Stay interested in everything around you, from the environment to politics.

- Live each day to the fullest.
- Make friends with people you respect. They will influence your quality of life.
- Stay active.
- Eat right.
- Don't waste time worrying about things you can't control, but make an impact where you can.
- Live within your means so that your money can last and you can remain independent.

Losing My Four-Legged Best Friend

Lesson: *"Out of something sad can come something good as long as we look for something bigger than ourselves."*
–Kathy Lynn

I was blessed to have the unconditional love of my Gatsby Dog for almost eighteen years, so when people tell me about the loss of a pet, I understand the pain. Most animal lovers do. In fact, when Gatsby Dog was about sixteen, my mother said she hoped that she died before he did because she wouldn't be able to cope with his passing and my grief.

My mother got what she asked for. She passed away in April 2006, and my furry soul mate, a 5-pound Yorkshire terrier named Kathy's Great Gatsby, died exactly one year and nine days later on April 12, 2007. He was almost eighteen, which is old for a dog. But for those of us whose dogs and cats are part of the family, they are never around long enough. I once read that God knew what he was doing when he capped the canine and kitty life spans at about twenty years. It was so they would always be taken care of by their owners. That might be right, but it did nothing to help ease my broken heart.

I can vividly remember the day I first set eyes on Gatsby Dog. It was in Houston, Texas, and I was shopping in a mall. There had been a fire at my home, and in it I had lost my little dog Ralph that had been with me for ten years. The last thing I was thinking of was another dog, but something drew me into the pet shop in Greenspoint Mall. It was love at first sight, and I knew I would never be truly happy without him.

Gatsby moved with me five times and was probably as well-traveled as most people. I was once married to an airline employee, and everywhere I went, the Gatsby Dog went. We were hardly ever apart, and when we were, my mother always took care of him. He had never spent a night without one of us until his illness forced him into intensive care right before he passed away.

Our animals give us such joy and love, especially those of us who don't have children or family living nearby. Gatsby and I shared travels, parties and many Mardi Gras parades in New Orleans. There is even a dog parade called Barkus in which he and I regularly participated. Each year we would have such fun picking out our themed costumes at a little shop in the French Quarter.

Right after Hurricane Katrina, we didn't know if there would be a Mardi Gras, but sure enough there was. That year's Barkus theme was perfect and my favorite: "There's No Place Like Home." I dressed as Dorothy, and Gatsby, of course, was the best Toto there. In fact, we were so good that CNN took video of us and ran it for a couple of days. I had no idea we had made it on TV until a friend from Las Vegas called to ask me if that was me in the Dorothy outfit. Of course, she recognized Gatsby right away. My mother and family and friends got such a kick out of this.

Gatsby went blind during his last year, but he dealt with it like a champ. He learned his way around the house and trusted me completely when we took daily walks around the block in our

historic Algiers Point neighborhood.

I almost lost Gatsby right after we traveled to Virginia for my mother's funeral. The veterinarian, Dr. Catherine, said that because of his age, any future plane trips would be too hard on him. So he was permanently grounded. I can remember being in a meeting at work one evening at about 6 p.m. We had just started when I got a call from Dr. Catherine telling me that I'd better drive out to her office in LaPlace, about forty-five minutes from New Orleans. I can remember running out of the meeting and praying the entire drive that Gatsby would be alive when I got there. I spent that night with him on the floor of the visiting room, and he pulled through. The next day I returned at lunch, and I remember thinking there was no way I could lose him so soon after losing my mom. I took him outside the veterinary hospital and sat on the ground and talked with God.

I said, "God, please don't take him right now. I just can't deal with it now. I want you to heal him, Lord. I beg you to heal him."

I laid my hands on his back and asked God to heal him. Then I took him back inside, kissed him goodbye, and drove back to work in New Orleans.

That night, Dr. Catherine called me to say that she didn't know what was going on, but the Gatsby Dog was getting stronger by the hour, had just eaten for the first time in two days, and was begging for more. I knew my prayer had been answered, and I thanked God for a little more time. I got exactly one more year of Gatsby's joy and love.

Gatsby's eventual passing was also a blessing because it happened peacefully. He had not been eating well for a couple of days, so Dr. Catherine told me to bring him in to see her the next day. That night I went to a friend's birthday party, but something kept telling me to leave and go home…that little voice that we should always listen to. Thank God I did.

When I arrived home Gatsby was asleep. I changed clothes and went to his bed; he heard me and woke up. I took him in my arms, and he kissed my face. My boyfriend was working on a cruise ship at the time, and he had called and left a message for me and one for Gatsby. I played the message, and Gatsby kissed the phone. I was carrying him back to his bed when all of the sudden he raised his front legs over his head and breathed a big sigh. And that was it. He passed away gently in my arms, just as I prayed he would.

The next day, I took him to be cremated, and it was one of the toughest things I have ever done. I handed him to the lady, but I called her back three times before I was finally able to let him go.

I went into a deep depression afterward and didn't even realize it. But everyone around me did. I couldn't think straight and was just totally out of it for about a month. Everything in my life was a blur. I would sit at Gatsby's bed each night and cry. Finally, my friend Joe called me one night and said, "So, Kathy Lynn, what are you going to do to celebrate Gatsby Dog's life? He was so special. You have to do something really special. A New Orleans-style second line or something."

Joe doesn't know it, but he saved me that day. I was now focused, and I had a purpose that included the Gatsby Dog. I began planning a funeral service for him that would long be remembered in New Orleans. In fact, I think he is the first dog to have such an event held in his honor. Friends and neighbors got involved with much anticipation and excitement. We decided to make it a tribute to Gatsby Dog and to anyone who had lost a beloved pet.

One of my friends, a pastor, held the service at the Canal Street-Algiers Ferry location on the Mississippi River levee. After the service, about forty costumed dogs and sixty people carrying the traditional second-line umbrellas followed the pastor and a jazz

band in a lively procession down the levee. Everyone paid tribute to the little Yorkie who was known throughout the neighborhood of Algiers Point. We ended up with a full party and wake celebration, just like you would have for a best friend at the neighborhood bar.

The event received media attention and was picked up nationally. The great news is that May 17, 2009, marked the Third Annual Gatsby Dog Second Line Parade in New Orleans, and the Louisiana SPCA promoted the event to help raise money for its shelter animals. It has also become a time each year when people can honor the passing of their pets.

So out of something sad has come something wonderful that keeps the Gatsby Dog's memory alive.

I have since been adopted by two little kittens, sisters Lily and Summer, who were abandoned at an office complex. They have brought unconditional love back into my life, and for that I am thankful.

Learnings:

- At the toughest times in our lives, friends and community are so important in helping us deal with our grief.
- Out of something sad can come something good if we look for something bigger than ourselves.
- God does answer prayers when we have faith.

Lesson 4 Questions

What are you passionate about in life?

How much time do you spend making others feel special each week? How could you go about doing that more?

Charles Gillam (left)

Connie, Claudius & Flea

Almost-Tina Turner, Hollie Vest

Yvonne Sharpe

Jo and Fritz Harsdorff

Amanda Overmyer

Ms. Irene Burrus

Carolina Gallop

Gatsby

Mr. Mardi Gras, Blaine Kern

Glenn (Michelle)

B.B. St. Roman

LESSON 5

SPIRITUAL CONNECTIONS, BELIEFS AND FRIENDS WILL GET YOU THROUGH LIFE'S CHANGES

"All who call on God in true faith, earnestly from the heart, will certainly be heard, and will receive what they have asked and desired."

Martin Luther

God, If I Am In A Dream, Please Wake Me Up!

Lesson: *"You have to put your complete faith in God. Everything is transient, and nothing lasts forever."*

–Connie and Claudius Fincher with their Beloved Pet, Flea
New Orleans

Before Hurricane Katrina, Connie and Claudius lived on St. Peter Street near the Bayou St. John area of New Orleans. They prepared for the storm by buying extra canned goods and other supplies, but like a lot of people, they thought the storm was headed to Florida. They decided to ride it out at their home.

They recounted what it sounded like Monday at 6 a.m. when the hurricane actually hit. All communications were down, so they had no way of knowing how much damage had been done. Other than some torn siding, their house appeared to have weathered the storm. In fact, it seemed as if the worst was over. Connie's two brothers came to check on them and decided to spend the night.

It was the next day that the water started to rise. Initially, they weren't concerned. During a bad storm the water would usually come up as high as their second or third front porch step and then be gone by the next morning. This time, however, was different. The water continued to rise. Because they could not get news reports, they had no idea that levees had failed. Instead of the water being gone the next morning, it was higher and coming in the front door. Connie's oldest brother waded three blocks in the deep water to see if he could find anyone and get some information. He came back with stories of looting and people gone crazy.

At that point, they decided they had to leave. They walked slowly in the waist-deep water, with Claudius' beloved dog, Flea, riding on his shoulders. They saw boats, but they were all full. The group became afraid and turned back home.

The next morning they decided to try again, as the water was continuing to rise and Connie could not swim. The men pulled her in a plastic bin that served as a makeshift boat, and the group set out once more.

Along the way they saw some people who told them to go to a nearby apartment complex called the American Can Company. They said from there, people were being transported to safety. They continued on, praying for safe passage.

"We walked and prayed, and God took care of us," Connie said.

They made it to the Can Company, filthy from wading in the dirty water. Flea remained on Claudius' shoulders the entire time. Eventually a helicopter landed, and the pilot got out and helped them board. He then disappeared into the apartment building.

On the aircraft was a woman and her son who said that they had been to the Superdome and it was chaotic. The woman and boy had made their way back to the Can Company in a last-ditch effort to escape the city and its madness.

The pilot reappeared, this time followed by a nurse and seven patients who had come to the Can Company from a nearby hospital. The pilot ordered all of the men out of the helicopter and replaced them with the patients. Only Connie, the woman and her son were allowed to stay.

Connie and Claudius assumed the helicopter would be back soon to pick up the men, so they said goodbye thinking that they would see each other shortly. As the aircraft rose above the city, the enormity of what had happened became apparent, and it shook Connie to her core.

"I got in the air and saw the entire city under water," she said. "I said, 'God if I am in a dream, please wake me up!'"

The group was flown to the nearby city of Slidell, where

Connie was able to take a shower and wash the stink off her body. She immediately started to ask when her husband would arrive.

"Slidell was torn up, too, and there was no drinkable water," Connie said. "They brought us bottled water to drink and gave us clothes. I was so worried about Claudius and Flea, not knowing where they were, or if they had gone back home, or what had happened to them."

Six days after Connie arrived in Slidell, a volunteer named Patty helped her locate Claudius. He and Connie's older brother had been taken to San Antonio, Texas. Connie's younger brother had stayed in New Orleans with Flea because the dog was not allowed on the aircraft.

Connie was so distraught about being separated from Claudius and her older brother that Patty finally drove her all the way to San Antonio to find them. The men were living in a shelter, and Connie's older brother was very sick. Connie assumed that the three days he spent in the dirty water caused his illness. He couldn't travel, and even if he could, getting around San Antonio was difficult. Connie said the city was full of Katrina evacuees who were "acting badly." It was truly a mess.

Patty and the shelter staff helped Connie and Claudius get transportation to Claudius' mother's home in Chicago until things got better in New Orleans. Connie's brother stayed in San Antonio and was placed in hospice, where he was diagnosed with liver cancer. He passed away on Oct. 24, 2005, at the age of sixty-six. Connie flew back to San Antonio and had her brother cremated. She planned to take his ashes back home to New Orleans so that they could have a service.

Eventually, Connie and Claudius returned to New Orleans to a rental home in the Algiers neighborhood. In the aftermath of the storm, Connie's younger brother had been forced to evacuate and

leave Flea behind, so Connie and Claudius began searching for the dog. They called Pet Finders and worked with several other groups, but had no luck. Then they met a volunteer group and gave them Flea's photo.

"Claudius begged them to find his baby," Connie said. "Claudius was driving everyone crazy without Flea. Flea is his baby."

Within two weeks the group found a dog that they thought was Flea living as "Rocko" with a family in Virginia. They showed Connie and Claudius an Internet photo, and the couple instantly recognized the dog as theirs.

The LA/SPCA helped Connie and Claudius get an attorney to handle all of the processing for free. The organization told them that the Virginia couple and their son would bring the dog back to New Orleans.

On the day Flea was to arrive, Claudius and Connie went to the airport baggage claim expecting him to be delivered in a kennel. While they were waiting, Claudius heard a familiar bark. When he turned around, Flea was running straight toward him. He was a little skinnier, but it was definitely Flea! The Virginia family could tell by the dog's reaction that he belonged with Connie and Claudius. Connie told him to dance and he stood up on his hind legs and did the little dance they had taught him as a puppy. Everyone was overjoyed. And Flea had become a celebrity.

"Now people know Flea before they know us," Connie said. "We meet a lot of nice people because of Flea. We sure are glad to have him home."

Learnings:

- You must put your complete faith in God. Everything is transient; nothing lasts forever.

- The love of God works through people.
- Connie and Claudius learned how to be more tolerant of other people, and they developed an inner peace from the experience.
- It doesn't pay to get upset about things that you can't take with you.
- When you hear that a storm is coming, get out!
- Connie learned from her guardian angel, Patty, that there are wonderful people in this world who give selflessly. Patty was not afraid, even when Connie was. God worked through Patty, and gave her the confidence to do what she did.

Living Through World War II

Lesson: *"Trust yourself and the person you love."*
–Jerry, 86
New Orleans

Jerry was an only child who graduated college and wanted to be a theatrical director until she married at age twenty. She was in Oregon working on a show when her boyfriend, Al, arrived at her door one night to tell her he had come to marry her and take her back home to Kansas City. They were married three days later and remained happily married for fifty-four years.

"The most dramatic change that happened to me occurred during World War II when Pearl Harbor was bombed," Jerry said. "I remember it vividly. It was a Sunday, and I had been married for one year. We were living in Kansas City, Missouri, and I didn't even have to discuss it with my husband. I knew he was going. He went down on Monday morning to enlist, and by Wednesday he was gone. It was two-and-a-half years before I set eyes on him again."

Al took a train to San Diego where he was put in a queue and given a number. His was 15, and his good friend's was 16. The

enlisted men were assigned to a ship according to when they arrived. The first ship only needed fourteen men, which ended up being a blessing. That vessel was bombed and everyone on board was lost.

Al served in the military for four years, and he came home only once.

"I never doubted that he would return to me," Jerry said. "I knew he would."

For the trip home, Al and his friend, who had served with him the entire time, were going to be put on different planes. They absolutely refused to be separated, and again it was a blessing. The plane that only had room for one of them went down in the ocean, and the passengers and crew were lost.

I asked Jerry how she and Al coped with the long separation.

"We wrote daily to one another," she said. "We never missed a day. That is what kept us both going for those four long years. Also being close to my family. And my job kept me busy. I worked eight hours a day at a war plant. I carpooled with five other ladies, and we were all in the same circumstance, so we had a lot to share on our one-hour drive to work each day. Those conversations helped a lot to know that everyone was going through the same thing. Also, several couples divorced and didn't make it through the war. It was very tough on people being separated that long. Think about it – no e-mail, no TV. We made, I think, two phone calls the entire time. So we wrote and wrote and wrote. That was our lifeline to each other. It was therapeutic for both of us. That is what kept us connected."

Learnings:

- Jerry's religion kept her focused and gave her purpose in life.
- She learned to rely on her faith in her husband, knowing that he was faithful and waiting for her, just as she was waiting for him.

- A hang-in-there attitude kept her going while her husband was away at war. She kept busy, knowing that their separation would eventually end.
- Trust yourself and the person you love.
- Loneliness is a burden. Surround yourself with friends of all ages.

Serious Illness Brings Lifestyle Changes, Stronger Spirituality

Lesson: *"Lean on your faith. Understand that there is a master plan and go with it."*

–Marcia Ensley, Mother, Wife, Business Executive
Tampa, Florida

Marcia, her husband Jack and their two children had lived in the Midwest for more than thirty years. Their relatives were more than a thousand miles away, but the couple's good jobs kept them in Indiana. They had always dreamed of spending their retirement in a warmer climate, and they ended up making the move much earlier than planned.

When Jack was diagnosed with colon cancer in 2006, their world came crashing down. Marcia said they were absolutely devastated until she decided one day that the pity party was over. A self-proclaimed control freak, Marcia realized she had to take charge.

The couple decided that Jack's illness was not going to beat them. Marcia started gathering all of the information she could find. She poured over books and medical Web sites. Marcia soon discovered WebMD and began reading information and exchanging e-mails with people who had been in their situation. Through Jack's first year of treatment, the family remained in the Midwest, but his illness accelerated their decision to move.

When the time came, they began researching places to live, schools for the children and health-care facilities for Jack. They ended up choosing the Tampa area.

It was a total leap of faith, and Marcia said she relied heavily on her spiritual beliefs. She realized that the situation was bigger than her. She acknowledged that there was a master plan for their lives, and that it would all work out in the end if she just trusted in God and went with the flow.

While they had no family in Tampa and had not even visited the city, Marcia said they felt it was where they were supposed to be. This instinct proved to be good. Their neighbors became like an extended family, and the schools, the medical care – everything was perfect for them.

The only real obstacle surfaced shortly after the move, and it involved Marcia's career. She had been with her company for twenty-three years and was seeking a transfer. But when she got to Florida, she found that the only available position would require an hour and a half commute each way. After fighting the decision, she finally gave up on staying with the company. A few months later, she received a job offer from an associate company that would allow her to work from home. At last, she had the perfect arrangement.

Three months later, they found out Jack's cancer was back, making Marcia's new job seem like even more of a godsend. It allowed her the flexibility to be there for him.

"Things didn't happen like I planned," she said, "but everything worked out according to God's plan."

As for Jack's medical care, the couple didn't feel comfortable with the first doctor they visited in Florida. The doctor was bluntly negative, telling them that Jack had only about two years to live. The doctor gave Jack and Marcia no hope, so they began searching for someone else. Marcia prayed for God to lead them to a good doctor

who would provide the treatment and support they needed.

Marcia compiled a list of private practitioners, and as she went through the pages, one name kept popping out at her, so she wrote it down. She remembered that the mother of one of her son's classmates was a nurse, and Marcia called her to get a recommendation. Surprisingly, she gave Marcia the same name she had written down. Marcia knew it was meant to be.

When they met the doctor for the first time, he was perfect. He was caring, optimistic and a wonderful communicator. As they were preparing to leave his office, a nurse asked how they had found him. Marcia told her about the referral. The nurse smiled. "God sends all his patients here," she said.

That was three years ago, and Jack's cancer is now in remission.

"There is a story I read that my situation reminds me of," Marcia said. "A little boy always sat at his mother's feet looking up at the underside of the picture she was embroidering. It looked pretty messy from his vantage point. I think God works the same way. Sometimes our life or our situation looks like a mess from where we sit, but God sees the whole picture. He sees it from the top down and works everything together for good. We need to give our trust to God that there is a master plan, and it will all work out."

Learnings:

- Take charge of your own medical care; ask questions and demand answers of the people treating you.
- Ask friends for referrals to better care if you don't feel comfortable with your doctors.
- Find a support system, even if it's an Internet blog.
- Lean on your faith. Understand that there is a master plan, and go with it.

Ora Et Labora: Prayer And Work

Lesson: *"Hope and love are both nouns and verbs; faith is only a noun. Does that mean there's nothing to do when it comes to having faith? No. Go back to loving and hoping more, and your faith will grow."*

–Paul Longo, Husband and Former Benedictine Monk
New Orleans

Paul's mid-twenties to mid-thirties were spent praying and working in a Benedictine monastery, where he taught at a college run by the monks and administered their travel abroad program. He spent his spare time at an art studio, working in ceramics and woodcarving. His goal was to become an ordained priest and tenured member of the college faculty.

But on his way to accomplishing that goal, something amazing happened. While working to complete his doctorate, Paul met a woman named Ann. They talked a lot, and he found her challenging. She ignited his thinking. This would become a turning point in his life. Ann and Paul fell in love, and he ended up leaving the monastery to marry.

It was a huge change for Paul, as his entire life had been devoted to religion. He found himself leaving the only life he had ever known.

Paul sought out a therapist to help him make sense of the change, and he also relied heavily on two friends whose cultural backgrounds and interests gave them unique perspectives on religion and love. One was from Iran and the other was a German American with Native American roots. Together, the three friends would explore life, poetry, nature and humanity through conversations that would last for hours on end.

Paul said these deep conversations about mystical Persian traditions helped him understand the concept of "sohbet," which he said is a connection resulting from the practice of deep and enlightened listening. He credits his friends with helping him recognize true love when it came along. Through words, a union was formed. Through dialogue, Paul found his soul mate.

Learnings:

- Paul's change led to the discovery of internal resources and an awareness of both the teacher and the student inside him.
- He learned to cherish questions more than answers. He said the formation of a good question gets your heart and soul involved in the process.
- He learned the difference between emptiness and fullness, and said sometimes it is better to be empty.
- People feel trapped when they are not thinking creatively. Use logic and every available resource to find options.
- Hope and love are both nouns and verbs; faith is only a noun. Does that mean there's nothing to do when it comes to having faith? No, go back to loving and hoping more, and your faith will grow.

Spouse's Death Triggers Loss Of Faith

Lesson: *"I am still struggling with my religious beliefs. I have come to believe that people are responsible for people."*

–Polly
Lafayette, Indiana

Polly's interview was a turning point for me. It was a very emotional meeting because Polly's story reminded me of my own losses. I came to realize how special these sessions were. People were willing to open up their hearts and pour out their feelings, and it was moving to be able to share their pain and triumphs.

Polly's most significant and devastating life change occurred when she was just thirty-seven. Polly was married to a wonderful

man named Steve who had always provided for her and their three children. She never had to think about financial matters or issues other than taking care of the kids and enjoying her family.

It happened so quickly! Her perfect world came tumbling down when Steve was diagnosed with Stage IV lung cancer. From March to September of that year, Polly's life was a blur. She busied herself day and night searching the Internet for the latest treatments and therapies. She consulted with doctors and nurses around the country. She read every cancer book she could get her hands on. She was the caretaker, and she focused all of her time and energy on her husband and trying to save him. They never discussed death, but she thinks that Steve knew he was dying and had stayed strong for her. He was always upbeat and positive about finding a cure, but she now realizes he was doing that for her. He knew that's what she needed at the time – hope. Hope that she would not lose him.

Steve passed away exactly six months from the day he was diagnosed.

"The hardest thing I ever had to do was to climb those steps in our house at 1 a.m. to wake my kids and tell them their father was gone," Polly said. "After that moment, I changed forever. I knew without a doubt that my strength could not be shaken by the day-to-day stresses of life. After that moment, I knew I could handle anything that life throws at me.

"I went through all the stages of grief that they say you go through, from depression to guilt. The biggest change after those four months was that I had nothing to do to stay busy, and it was a shock to my system. I had been in constant motion for six months, from managing our time, his diet and his medicine schedule, to doing absolutely nothing. I had nothing to do but grieve. It was a terrible void for me.

"I had a huge loss due to Steve's death that has also changed me forever. I lost my faith. My faith was strong when we were going through his illness. I grew up, lived life Catholic and didn't question much. All in the world was as it should be. God was taking care of things. My faith got me through the ordeal of losing my husband, but after his death, I found myself questioning the very existence of God. If there is a loving God, why does he allow so many people to suffer?

"Seeing Steve suffer and then walking on the cancer ward and looking at all of these other people suffering and their families suffering with them, I said to myself: Ain't nobody running this ship in that way. There is no grand plan. Everyone is not fine. To this day that is what I believe.

"I believe there may be some spiritual thing, but not an omnipotent God. We were put here, and what happens just happens. The thing is, I would give up everything and go live in a tent if I could get back the faith that I had. It was so comfortable. I miss that feeling of peace I always had growing up and through most of my adulthood.

"I am still struggling with my religious beliefs. I have come to believe that people are responsible for people. That is why I have joined the Sierra Club, become politically active and pushed my children to do the same and to help others."

Learnings:

- Steve's death allowed Polly to learn how to accept help from others – not financial help, but small things like someone picking up the kids or dropping off a cooked meal. Polly had always felt she should be self-sufficient, but Steve's passing made her realize how important it is to accept kindness from others and to be there for others when they are in need.
- Going from a partnership to being a single parent is tough, but it can be done. The most important thing is to make sure you are there for your children, teaching them and helping them to cope – especially

during the early years.

- Don't settle for the easy choices. Ask yourself what is the right thing to do and do it, even if it's tough and people criticize you.

My Spirituality

Lesson: *"I believe that God sent experiences and people into my life that strengthened my faith and brought me closer to Him."*
–Kathy Lynn

I can remember my mother taking me and my sister to church every Sunday. We grew up Baptist, but later in life I attended the Catholic Church with my husband. I have since explored several other religions.

My best friend, Mary Crews, influenced me greatly when I was a child. Mary's family moved in next door to mine when I was in second grade and she was in third. Her father was a minister and the entire family was devout. In addition to attending church each Sunday morning with my mother, I began going with Mary on Wednesdays and Sunday nights.

We also attended summer bible school and two weeks of summer bible camp. Usually we went to a camp in Tennessee called Bancroft Bible Camp, but one year we traveled to a camp in Georgia, which was a special treat.

One night at camp, just as we were all getting ready to go to sleep, I began to cry. When the counselor asked me what was wrong I told her that I was sad that my dad was not a Christian. The other girls started crying too and began talking about people in their families. We ended up having a night of prayer for our families and friends. The spirit of God was with us and brought us together in a special way that I am sure none of us has ever forgotten.

During my marriage and shortly after my divorce I went through the motions of practicing my religion, but I was not as engaged as I am now. What changed? I believe that God sent experiences and people into my life that strengthened my faith and brought me closer to Him.

The experiences are ones that I have written about in other chapters of this book: the blessing of having my mother healed from a sickness and being able to enjoy her for just a little longer; the experience of God giving me an additional year with my beloved Gatsby Dog.

A gentleman named Matt who came to New Orleans to work on the recovery after Hurricane Katrina also had a profound impact on my spiritual life. After the devastation of the storm, conversations with him and with other friends about the meaning of life deepened my relationship with God. Matt became my personal spiritual coach, sharing thoughts, books and meditation techniques with me.

I now spend time each morning with God. I read spiritual articles, the Bible and books such as Joel Olsteen's *Your Best Life Now*. I have underlined several passages in this book and review them daily during my time with God. I pray and meditate on positive affirmations for my life and the lives of my friends and family.

I also have learned to pause midday and meditate. Sometimes it's only for a couple of minutes, but it refocuses my entire day and brings me peace.

Recently I mentored a friend who was going through lots of change in his life. Through this experience of sharing with him, I have strengthened my own spirituality. The old saying of "When we help others, we help ourselves" is so true.

Learnings:

- Make time for yourself and your spirituality every day.
- Meditation helps refocus your day.
- When we use our learnings to help others, we are blessed because we become stronger ourselves.

Lesson 5 Questions

What is one of the worst things that could happen to you, and how would you deal with it? Who would be around to assist/comfort you?

What are your spiritual connections in life? Do you take time each day for God or your spiritual beliefs? If not, how can you change your daily schedule to make the time?

LESSON 6

PURSUE YOUR DREAMS, NO MATTER WHAT

"Go confidently in the direction of your dreams. Live the life you have imagined."

Henry David Thoreau

The People I Have Met Continue To Shape My Life

Lesson: *"When things happen in your life, they are all connected. Let your life flow, and the right things usually always happen."*
–Charles Gillam, Self-Taught Folk Artist
New Orleans' Lower 9th Ward

Charles grew up right down the street from Fats Domino and played with his kids. Religion played a key role in Charles' life. His mother was part Native American and his father was African American. Charles' parents were always taking him to visit different churches, exposing him to everything from Native American beliefs to Voodoo. Charles and his family were members of a Christian church, and he said his parents took great pains to teach him right from wrong.

Growing up in the Lower 9th Ward, Charles was poor, but he didn't let that get in the way of his progress. At a young age he discovered his love of art and working with his hands, and he would spend hours taking objects apart and putting them back together.

Charles always wanted to better himself, and at age thirteen he and his brother began going to the French Quarter to make money by shining shoes. Charles had learned Louisiana history in school, but it was his time spent in the Quarter that brought this history to life for him. He would watch the Jackson Square artists paint portraits and street scenes, and it absolutely fascinated him. He would stand for hours and watch each stroke of the brush as another creation took shape.

The Quarter was filled with all colors and types of people, and Charles' life began to be influenced by those he met there. There were the smartly dressed business people who were his customers and encouraged his success, as well as the artists who took him under

their wings and taught him to use his God-given talent.

Charles' transformation from shoe-shiner to artist began in earnest when a painter by the name of Claude Doucette gave him his first set of brushes. Claude was a regular on the square, and he helped Charles hone his skills.

Charles soon began to venture into the city's scenic Garden District and Uptown neighborhoods by streetcar and on his bike. It was there that he met artist Johnny Cash, a rotund old man who painted and sculpted while his constant companions – two spider monkeys – sat perched on his shoulders. Johnny hired young Charles to help him mix his plaster, and Charles spent months working with and learning from him. Charles then ventured further uptown, where he met an artist named Willie White who would put his paintings on his front porch to dry. Charles befriended Willie and was inspired.

Charles said a variety of other people influenced him. There was the Italian man from Sicily who started his own bleach company and taught Charles about business. There was Joann Clevenger, an art patron and New Orleans restaurant owner; and artist George Rodrique of Blue Dog fame, who gave Charles the easel that he still paints on today in his folk art gallery in the Algiers neighborhood.

Charles feels that God put him in contact with these people for a reason. He has learned from all of them, and they have helped him help others.

Charles and his wife, Susan, are now working with the young African-American children who live in the historic Algiers area. By teaching them art and spending time with them during the summer months and after school, Charles and Susan feel they have an opportunity to exert a positive influence. Charles hopes to point the neighborhood children in the right direction, and to help shape their lives the way so many people took the time to shape his.

Learnings:

- Be persistent; don't let anything hold you back from trying to do what you want to do.
- Try to do the right things, and be careful about what you ask God for. You usually get it, and you need to be alert when it comes.
- When things happen in your life, they are all connected. Let your life flow, and the right things will usually happen.
- Be honest and loyal to others and to yourself.
- Treat people the way you want to be treated. Remember that love always conquers hate.
- Leave something behind for others.

Almost-Tina Turner

Lesson: *"Have a purpose and reason to be excited to get up every morning. Do the very best you can with whatever it is you're doing."*

–Hollie Vest, Entertainer and Business Owner
Las Vegas and New Orleans

Music and entertaining have been part of Hollie's life since she was a little girl. She started singing and performing for friends and family at the age of three, and then singing with vocal groups as a teen. In her early twenties, Hollie signed several recording contracts as a solo artist and with a female trio called Mello, Chill, & Shock. *Billboard* magazine compared them to The Supremes, and their song "Feel the Music" made it to the Top 100 on the pop chart. After the group broke up, Hollie formed her own band and worked in Los Angeles hotels, restaurants and nightclubs successfully for fifteen years. During that time, Hollie also wrote, recorded and produced a compilation of original songs entitled *The Thrill of the Hunt*.

Hollie's goal was to live out her dream of becoming a famous

recording artist, writing and singing her own songs. Then something happened that changed her career.

It started when Hollie was singing with her band. Whenever she would perform a rock-and-roll song, she would always be compared to Tina Turner, even though she wasn't singing Tina Turner songs.

This happened so often that in 1984 she added two Tina Turner songs – "What's Love Got To Do With It" and "Private Dancer" – to her repertoire. The requests for her to sing more Tina became so numerous that on New Year's Eve 1984, without telling the band why, she asked them to play "What's Love" at midnight. As the music began, Hollie appeared on stage dressed as Tina, from her wig and attitude down to her high heels. The show brought the house down. Almost-Tina was born that night, and Hollie's career was transformed.

"People give and show me their love and admiration for Tina," Hollie said. "Tina is such a wonderful inspiration to so many women, and even men. Tina is respected and admired for so many reasons. However, sometimes the emotions of her fans can be quite overwhelming. The real stars have paid a heavy price for their careers, and that price is privacy. I don't know how they deal with such intense fame and recognition on a daily basis."

Hollie took her wildly successful Tina tribute on the road, appearing throughout the U.S. and Canada, and in Africa, Asia and Europe. She also made appearances on cruise ships.

"Looking back, I am so happy that I am not that rock star, but I can just be Hollie," she said. "Yet at the same time, I get to experience that exhilaration when I perform as Tina. As it turns out, I get to enjoy the best of both worlds. I have my privacy, and I have the excitement of being a rock star when I do my Tina tribute."

In 2000, Hollie published a book on the subject of celebrity impersonators and tribute artists entitled, "Made You Look: Who Do You Look Like?"

In 2001, Hollie moved to New Orleans and renovated a historic mansion. She opened it as Magnolia Mansion, a small boutique hotel and wedding and special events venue.

In 2005, Hurricane Katrina hit, and life changed forever for so many people. Magnolia Mansion was vandalized in the aftermath of the storm, and much of the beautiful furniture and most of Hollie's personal and business belongings were destroyed. But she picked up the pieces and reopened as soon as she could to help house people returning to the city to rebuild. The experience changed the way she felt about material things, and Hollie made lifelong friends, some of whom never would have crossed her path were it not for the storm. It also taught her that she is stronger and even more tenacious than she ever imagined.

In 2007, Hollie made another dream come true with the world premiere of THRILLUSIONS®, a musical Las Vegas-style show at Harrah's Casino in New Orleans, in which she performed as Almost-Tina.

In November 2007, Hollie and her mother put Magnolia Mansion up for sale so that they could spend more time together. Hollie has repaired and restored the property and says it is time for someone else to enjoy its grandeur and take it to the next level of success.

"I will always love New Orleans, but now is the time for me to take care of those I love and miss, and perform while I still can," she said. "I am prepared to let go and move on, but will always come back to visit those I love in New Orleans. Like many others who leave, we always return. For now, I know with all my heart that it is time for me to move on."

Learnings:

- Hollie said she will always love to sing and entertain people and make them happy. Performing is in her blood, and it's what she loves to do best. She is happiest when on stage.
- Hollie has learned that privacy is also important to her. Performing as a character or doing tribute shows allows her both the peace of privacy and the pleasure of performing.
- Don't take yourself too seriously and never lose your sense of humor. A sense of humor is the best medicine, especially during hard times.
- Perseverance, persistence and resilience are important qualities, no matter what your goals and career demand of you.
- It's important to learn how to overcome obstacles and make a way when you think there is none. Don't think about what you can't do. Think about what is possible.
- Never lose faith or give up on what you believe in or what is truly your heart's desire.
- From Hurricane Katrina, Hollie learned that things are replaceable or reparable. It taught her that family and friends mean everything.
- Cherish those you love and protect them as best you can.
- Show kindness to someone every day. Even small acts of kindness can change someone's life.
- Don't be afraid to do something you have never done before. That is how we grow, become stronger and wise.
- Cultivate your purpose. Have a reason to be excited about waking up every morning, even if it's simply doing the very best you can with whatever it is you're doing.

His True Purpose In Life Is Revealed

Lesson: *"My epiphany came from a change I didn't choose."*

–Jon Racherbaumer, World-Renowned Magician
and Author of More than 60 Books
New Orleans

Jon worked for Eastern Airlines for twenty-seven years

before he found his real purpose in life. When he started with Eastern, he thought it would be a six-month job. But six months later, he had free travel benefits and was being trained in all facets of the organization, so he decided to stick with it.

Although the airline business provided great benefits and a sound retirement, Jon said it didn't nourish his soul. So in his spare time, he pursued his favorite hobby – magic. He has been passionate about magic since the age of ten.

Jon had what he describes as a religious experience when he attended his first magic show. As he explained to me in detail how he rushed home that day to tell his mom what he'd witnessed, he did so with the excitement of a ten-year-old boy. The awe, curiosity and inspiration associated with magic are still very much alive in Jon.

When the airline industry was deregulated in 1985, Jon got a handshake and early retirement from the company he thought he would work for until he retired. He had absolutely no idea what to do. After being with the same company for so long, the change was almost overwhelming.

Jon spent the first few weeks contemplating his loss, and after some thought, it became clear to him that he should see the situation as an opportunity. He said he realized that people can become embedded in their comfort zones, and the shock of sudden change can be difficult to handle.

This change that he hadn't chosen forced Jon to reinvent himself based on what he really knew and loved: magic, writing and reading. He soon began performing at local corporate and private parties, and now works all over the country. He has published more than sixty books on the subject of magic and illusions.

After his first engagement, he asked himself, "Why didn't I do this in the beginning?" The answer was the comfort zone. Had he

not been forced into early retirement, he would still be working with the airline and wouldn't have experienced the pure happiness that magic has brought to his life.

Learnings:

- One of our most important assets is our psychic equipoise or balance. We have to be like tightrope walkers in life. Life changes, such as job loss or relationship problems, can throw us off balance for a time, and it is important to know how to work through the changes quickly.
- Jon said times of upheaval are opportunities to reconsider and reassess our lives.
- When you go through a change that is forced upon you, look for the opportunity it presents rather than focus on the loss.
- Most people fear change. Be willing to take risks and test your strengths and weaknesses.
- Jon said he has learned more from his failures than from his successes. Don't be afraid to fail.
- Learn to appreciate mystery for its power to energize us and keep us curious about ourselves and the world around us. Embrace the wonder of not knowing.

Soul Mates Working Together For 20 Years

Lesson: *"Don't be afraid to change."*
–Philippart and Anja, Performers
Holland

Philippart and Anja truly meet the definition of soul mates. During our interview they would finish each other's sentences, and they had that special unspoken communication that one would expect from performers who have worked together for more than twenty years.

Three seemed to be their magic number. They first met in

1985, but it would be three years before they worked together, three more years before they became business partners, and another three years before they became life partners.

Anja is a dancer and Philippart is a singer and magician. They met through a mutual friend who told Philippart what a great performer Anja was and suggested that he add her to his act. Philippart called Anja, and they met to discuss the possibility of working together. Anja was impressed with Philippart, but she didn't want to be anyone's assistant, and she told him so. For Philippart, it was love at first sight.

When the two began working together, their lives changed completely and dramatically. They were on the same wavelength, but it was difficult to merge their acts. They decided to start from scratch, with Anja designing some costumes and Philippart creating new illusions.

They had very little money, but with their savings they bought props. They recorded their own music, and eventually their show began to take shape. They argued a lot back then. They didn't know what they were talking about or how to communicate with one another, and they described themselves as very insecure. In reality, the characters for what was to be their hit show were being developed, and they didn't even realize it.

The characters evolved slowly during the first two years. The couple had seen the movies *Indiana Jones* and *Batman*, and both had inspired big ideas. The show began to take shape. Philippart and Anja painted their faces in garish colors to exaggerate their expressions. They crafted a unique and stylized way of moving with *Beetle Juice*-type music as a soundtrack. And they took old-fashioned, vintage illusions and made them unique. At the time, Philippart and Anja didn't realize what they had created, but that changed when they performed at a magic convention and received a standing ovation

from a room full of magicians.

"Boom, it hit us," Philippart said. "We had a hit!"

Now, they appear across Europe and even appeared in New Orleans for their first U.S. performance.

"We feel the world is our home," said Philippart. "We have traveled all over the world sharing our magic show with wonderful crowds."

"We are now an entity," said Anja. "We have become one. We have more freedom. It is enormous. We go when and where we want, but we never leave each other behind."

Learnings:

- Keep an open mind, especially to people from other countries. Respect their values and learn why they do things the way they do.
- If you have no prejudices, you will have a richer life. Then the world becomes a treasure chest – dive in and you can get as rich as you want!
- Spend time communicating with and trying to understand your partner. Keeping an open mind is the foundation of a successful relationship.
- Don't be afraid to change. Most people are afraid to get out of their box.

From The Little Fat Girl In The Sears Dressing Room To Woman Body Builder

Lesson: *"There is no perfect body. It is better to be strong and healthy than to look like some skinny model that the magazines tell us we should look like. Feel blessed that you have your health."*
–Kathy Lynn

I vividly remember being a little ten-year-old girl in the Sears dressing room, and my mother telling me that I had graduated

to chubby sizes. I was horrified, and it made such an impact on me that it has stayed with me my whole life. Even when I was anorexic and weighed 89 pounds, I still saw myself as that chubby little girl in the Sears dressing room.

Of course, when my sister went through the same stage, everyone told her she was cute and she would get over it – and she did. Today, she is a size three or five compared to my size six or eight.

I have worked on my weight all of my life, and most of the time I have been slender – not skinny, but slender. Still, I always felt like that chubby girl in the dressing room. Maybe if my mom had changed my diet and exercise routine and basically let me go through the chubby phase, I might have grown out of it as my sister did – but who knows? My mother did the best she could. She took me to a doctor who put me on a diet and gave me diet pills. Even though I was only ten years old, in those days, that was ok. We didn't realize that what I was being given was what people in the 1970s called "speed," and that they paid large amounts for those little speckled pills.

My weight fluctuated for the next couple of years until I discovered boys in the seventh grade and at age thirteen became a cheerleader. Twiggy was big in those days, and I thought I had to look like her. So I ate little more than a graham cracker and a Coke each day for about seven months, and my weight went from 120 to 89 pounds. I was anorexic and didn't even know such a condition existed. Thank God I had a happy ending and eventually started eating right again.

Since that time, I have pretty much managed to stay within five to seven pounds of my ideal weight, only spiking up a couple of times when I received a promotion at work and had to relocate to

a new area, with all of the stress that entails. And, of course, after Katrina. But every time I gained weight, I would always get a grip on myself and get back to my goal range.

During my Katrina exodus, I packed on ten pounds (everyone who went through it seems to have lost or gained ten pounds) and decided it was time to get myself in shape for life. After all, I was not exactly a spring chicken anymore. So on my own I lost twenty pounds by increasing my aerobic exercise and following a good basic and balanced diet over a ten-month period.

However, I wanted to feel stronger and really be in shape for life. Even though I lifted light weights three times a week and walked five days a week, it wasn't changing my body enough.

Enter Mark, a former Body for LIFE champion, and my life changed. Mark was in town to help with the hurricane recovery effort, and I met him through a friend. He offered to be my coach, and I talked two of my other friends into going through the Body for LIFE program with me. Mark worked with us in the gym daily and we followed the program for twelve weeks. At the end of that period I had lost about eight pounds, but the dramatic change was the inches lost. I had gone from size ten pants to a size six. Working with weights and doing the cardio differently and eating more protein really paid off for me.

I now have my Body for LIFE and I am sticking to the routine Monday through Friday. I let myself have cheat days on Saturday and Sunday. It works for me, and now I think I can finally say goodbye to that chubby, sad girl in the Sears dressing room. I hope to never meet her again. I have become a woman bodybuilder, and I love my body.

Learnings:

- There is no perfect body. It is better to be strong and healthy than to look like the skinny models that magazines tell us we should look like.
- The old adage of a balanced diet really works when combined with strength training and cardio work.
- Try not to obsess over weight. Enjoy life and stay active.
- Try different aerobic exercises such as biking and roller blading to keep your workouts interesting.
- Get an exercise partner who goes to the gym every day. It will motivate you to show up and not let them down.
- Reading books on fitness and exercise helps me stay focused on being fit.

Lesson 6 Questions

What have you dreamed about doing and not yet done?

Is there someone you know who is trying to fulfill a dream? Can you help them? Who are they, and how will you do this?

LESSON 7

NEVER GIVE UP: MANAGING THROUGH ALL LIFE THROWS AT YOU

"Good fortune and bad are equally necessary to man, to fit him to meet the contingencies of this life."

French Proverb

Losing Everything Can Be A Blessing In Disguise

Lesson: *"This is who I am now and what I do."*
–Fay Faron, from Private Eye in San Francisco to Author, Columnist and Community Activist in New Orleans

Talk about an interesting life. This lady has been on every talk show on TV, including three appearances on "Oprah." What was she talking about? A new career born of catastrophic life change.

In 1989, Fay was working as a TV producer and living in Sausalito, a cute little town across the bay from San Francisco. One Monday evening in November, her car had broken down and she was walking from the bus stop to her new houseboat. She had just gotten off the bus when a man approached her and asked for the time. Before she knew what was happening, the man punched her in the face and grabbed her purse with her credit cards, identification, driver's license and cash. Neighbors rushed her to the hospital and she was home the next day, nursing a very swollen face with a cut that required nine stitches.

While she was home recovering, she heard news reports of a storm with 90 mph winds brewing in the Pacific Ocean. Fay was alarmed, as her houseboat was right on the bay. The next evening the storm hit, and within ten minutes the waves were crashing against her home. The houseboat had open pontoons that quickly filled with six feet of water. Fay only had time to grab her dog and jump off as the houseboat and all of her worldly possession disappeared beneath the churning water.

Fay had lost everything but her dog and the clothes on her back. With the help of neighbors she was able to retrieve the boat, but it was waterlogged. Fay had no insurance and no place to live other than the soggy mess that was once her home.

Soon after, Fay and her boyfriend broke up, and she lost most of her friends because they were also his friends and employees. Of course, she still had her job, but she realized she was unhappy and longed for a change.

For the next six months Fay cried a lot, started drinking more, and sank into a deep depression. She was sitting at a bar one night when she realized things had to change. Being happy in life was at the top of her list, but it definitely wasn't happening. She decided to make a list of everything that was wrong – her car, her house, her job – and then do something about it. She put the car up for sale the next day, quit her job, and headed to Fiji for six weeks.

When Fay returned from her vacation, she called the man who had sold her the houseboat, which, she found out later, had been an accident waiting to happen. The man told her that the storm was an act of God, and her loss wasn't his problem. She replied that she had talked with God, and God advised her to hire an attorney.

Fay's attorney began aggressively pursuing the case. He said that in order to prove the houseboat was unsafe, he needed to find the person who had rented it before Fay bought it. As it turned out, the renter was someone who moved around a lot, but Fay was relentless and located him after just two days.

In the end, Fay won the case, and her attorney was so impressed with her investigative skills that he hired her to find people he needed on other cases.

And that is how her new career was born. Fay started the Rat Dog Dick Detective Agency and had an extremely successful twenty-five year career as a private investigator. She gained notoriety for cracking one of the biggest fraud schemes in the state of California, and she also became a syndicated columnist in Dallas and San Francisco. She became the spokesperson for private detectives nationally, appearing on every talk show from "Oprah" to "Larry King Live."

The next challenge came when she decided to leave San Francisco for New Orleans. Fay didn't know anyone in New Orleans, but she had visited the city several times over the years and loved it. On one visit, she rode the Canal Street Ferry across the Mississippi River to a little neighborhood called Algiers Point. She saw a for-sale sign and couldn't believe the cost of real estate compared to San Francisco. She realized that moving would mean she could be in a warm climate year-round, pay off a house, and be in a city she loved. So after living in San Francisco for twenty-five years, she relocated to the place she felt she was supposed to be.

Fay enjoyed anonymity in her new neighborhood, where no one knew her as a talk-show regular. She had no reputation to live up to and was free to reinvent herself. An associate suggested that she could make money by helping others do what she had been doing for years as a syndicated columnist. Fay agreed it was worth a shot. She is now earning a great income from her home office every day, and enjoying the warmth and fun of New Orleans.

Learnings:

- Take on change in manageable bites. Consider one problem at a time and figure out how to solve it to be happy.
- When Fay found herself going through tough times, she made up a phrase that she always goes back to when approaching change in her life: "This is who I am now and what I do."
- Fay credits her parents for giving her the love and security that fostered her can-do attitude.
- Look for the up side of loss. What positive can come out of it?

War As A Turning Point

Lesson: *"Poverty can lead a person into making poor choices. But opportunity and the means to do better can change his or her life forever."*
–Fritz Harsdorff, Retired Newspaper Editor
New Orleans

Fritz was born in 1925, right before the Great Depression, in the little South Texas town of Woodsboro. His father lost the family business in the Depression because he kept giving credit to people who couldn't pay, and Fritz and his family eventually went to live on a farm just outside the town. His family was destitute and Fritz hated the farm. He never saw anyone except on Sundays, when he went to town to visit his grandparents.

Young Fritz got into trouble at every turn even though his uncle was deputy sheriff. In one instance, he was out hunting with a friend and the two broke into an old farmhouse to eat some jelly because they were so hungry. Both ended up in jail.

When Fritz turned seventeen, he enlisted in the military to join his four older brothers in the war effort. Pearl Harbor had just been bombed, and he was now old enough to fight for his country. He signed up for the Navy and was sent to Houston. While the recruits were waiting in line to get their vaccinations, Fritz was singled out by the commanding officer, who wanted to make sure Fritz was old enough and strong enough to join. Fritz only weighed 115 pounds, but he assured the officer that he could handle the experience because he had worked on a farm most of his life. The officer shrugged and told him to get back in line.

After Fritz's enlistment, there was a huge parade with flags flying and crowds cheering for the men as they shipped off to Australia. Fritz had never felt so important in his life, and he wore his uniform with pride. It took thirty-six days to get to Australia, where Fritz saw kangaroos and other exotic wildlife. For a farm boy from Texas, it was quite an eye-opening experience. Fritz also marveled at having three meals a day and never having to go hungry. As someone who grew up in poverty, it was the first time he had ever had a daily breakfast.

Fritz was assigned to the USS Phoenix, and he spent three years in New Guinea, Borneo and the Philippines. He experienced ship-to-ship battles and witnessed the Japanese Kamikazes. He remembers hearing about the bombing of Japan while listening to the ship radio.

Fritz said his time in the military changed his life. He went from being a poor farm boy to being a world traveler who had lived through war. He said the Navy gave him the opportunity to take control of his life and destiny.

He did a second tour of duty during the Korean War as a journalist on the USS Indiana, and eventually became the editor of a military newspaper. That experience would lead to a lifelong love of journalism.

When Fritz returned home to the U.S., he took a part-time job at the newspaper in Kingsville, Texas, while attending college on the GI Bill. After graduation, he worked for three years in Corpus Christi, where he met and married his wife.

When a friend at the Corpus Christi paper moved to New Orleans, he called Fritz and talked him into moving, too. Fritz eventually became the associate editor of the New Orleans paper. He has served the community of New Orleans with the experience and knowledge he acquired because of a place called Pearl Harbor.

Learnings:

- Poverty can lead a person into making poor choices. But opportunity and the means to do better can change his or her life forever.

- Military service teaches responsibility and instills self-confidence.
- In leaving home and experiencing the wider world, we become more open as human beings.

Dealing With Serious Illness

Lesson: *"Get the stress out of your life, even if it means ending a relationship, quitting your job or whatever it takes to find peace."*

–James
California

James was celibate until he was twenty, when he had his first sexual experience with a man. It developed into a relationship that lasted for more than seven years.

James grew up in the Old South in a very conservative Baptist family. He was taught that homosexual relationships were sinful and wrong. He tried to be "normal," as his parents and religion dictated, but he knew from an early age that he was different. Still, he had girlfriends his entire school life and into college. They were never sexual relationships, but they were loving and close.

It was only after moving to California, away from the South and the influence of his parents and church, that he realized it was ok to be gay. He also spent a summer in Europe, where he became convinced that he was pretty darned normal.

James is comfortable with his life choice and has had two long-term relationships. He has also dated a few people in between.

James always practiced safe sex – at least he thought he had – and he made it a point to have a routine physical each year. One day, James' doctor called after his annual exam and left a message asking him to come into the office. James suspected immediately that he had contracted HIV. He remembers falling onto his bed after hearing the message and going numb, not being able to do anything but lie there in shock.

The next day, the visit to his doctor's office confirmed his fear. He was HIV-positive. While the doctor was supportive, James' psyche was in shambles. He decided to call on an old friend who had been diagnosed with HIV several years earlier. The friend flew to Los Angeles and spent the week with James, helping him come to terms with the illness. His friend told him that HIV was not a death sentence, but it was important to stay as healthy as he could and to get the right treatment.

The illness forced James to look at his life, and he decided that he had to eliminate all stress and put his health first. He called the manager of his company, told him the truth, and then resigned. He then started to look for other, stress-free ways to support himself.

After hearing why James had resigned, his former supervisor asked to meet with him. During the meeting, James learned that his boss had consulted with the company's corporate office and learned that James was eligible for disability. He could receive seventy percent of his compensation, and that would allow him to take care of himself, keep his benefits and focus all of his attention on staying healthy.

James felt that God had answered his prayers by allowing him to eliminate stress from his life. He decided to give back to his community, becoming an active volunteer for several organizations in the Los Angeles area.

Learnings:

- It's important to get professional coaching and psychological help when going through a serious illness.
- Remove as much stress from your life as you can, even if it means ending a relationship, quitting your job or whatever it takes to find

peace.

- Learn all you can about your illness, and be assertive with your doctors.
- Truly live in the moment. Travel and enjoy your life.
- Friends who accept you as you are are greater than any treasure. Give back to them.

Loss Of Child

Lesson: *"Realize that death is just part of life. Everyone goes through losses of loved ones. It's not easy, but live your life for the others who are left behind."*
–Ms. Irene Burrus
New Orleans

Ms. Irene, who was interviewed in another section of this book about her enthusiasm for life and aging gracefully, has also had her share of tragedy. When Ms. Irene was thirteen, she lost her mother. Decades later, she lost her own daughter, Marcia, to ovarian cancer. Marcia was just fifty-one.

Ms. Irene said the loss of her daughter at a relatively young age had the biggest impact on her, personally. Her daughter was diagnosed at age forty-one and fought ovarian cancer for ten years. She went through surgery and treatments during the first year and was told after five years that she was clear of the disease, only to have it return.

Ms. Irene said she was able to remain hopeful until the last six months of Marcia's life, when she saw her daughter deteriorating before her eyes. Marcia was such an inspiration to everyone around her, keeping an upbeat attitude until the very end. Finally, Marcia told Ms. Irene that she just couldn't live with the pain and suffering anymore. Ms. Irene thanked God for her merciful passing.

After Marcia's death, Ms. Irene sat at home for several days and cried. Then she decided, "I can sit and cry at home, or I can go out and live life and help my family that's left."

And that's exactly what she did. She was there for her daughter's children and for the rest of the family during that very difficult time. And she says never a day goes by that she does not think about Marcia.

When asked what she would tell others about losing a son or daughter she replied, "Realize it's just part of life. Everyone goes through losses of loved ones. It's not easy, but live your life for the others who are left behind."

Learnings:

- Life can change so quickly! It's not smooth. We all have tragedies in our lives.
- Appreciate your relationships. Ms. Irene said she was truly blessed to have been close to her daughter for fifty-one years.

Divorce Is Not An Option

Lesson: *"Love is not a feeling but a commitment. For better or worse, worse is going to happen. If you can get through the bad stuff, you will be stronger as a couple and as individuals."*

–Taylor
Arizona

Taylor met Michael on an Internet dating site. She was looking for a man who was a Christian, was close to her in age, and who would accept her as a single mother. She got two out of three – Michael is eleven years her senior. It is the second marriage for both. They are also an interracial couple.

When I spoke with Taylor, I asked if race had ever been an

issue for either of them. Her reply was unequivocal.

"We never look at it that way," she said. "We fell in love with each other, and we don't even think of our race. We also find that how we look at it is how others perceive it, too."

When I interviewed Taylor, she and Michael had been married for six years. They hit it off as soon as they met, and dated for six months before tying the knot. They endured the usual ups and downs of marriage, but things changed suddenly just after Michael turned fifty-five.

One day, Michael announced that he was no longer happy. After wrestling with the situation for about two weeks, he decided to move out. Even though Taylor was devastated, she thought the best thing to do was to let him go. Maybe he just needed some time to be alone.

The first few days without Michael were miserable. Taylor would e-mail him, sending daily inspirational thoughts on marriage and telling him she loved him. She said they had always promised each other that divorce was not an option. No matter what they had been through, they had made the commitment to marriage, and Taylor was determined to save it.

But after not hearing from him for some time, Taylor decided to move forward with the new arrangement. As fate would have it, she ran into a former boyfriend who asked her out to dinner. She accepted. They went on a couple of dates, and it was as if they'd never been apart. But in the back of her mind, Taylor could not forget Michael and their commitment to one another.

One morning, the boyfriend gave Taylor a ride to work. As she got out of the car, she leaned down to kiss him on the cheek and thank him for the ride. As she started walking toward the entrance, she spotted Michael's car. He was sitting and waiting for her, and

he had just seen her kiss another man. He immediately asked who the man was and what she was doing with him. She told him that because he had moved on, she was trying to do the same. That's all it took. Michael said he was ready to come home, and he asked her if she would take him back.

The couple reunited, but the first two weeks were tough. Taylor said they had to re-establish who they were as individuals and as a couple. They also had some in-depth discussions about the possibility of this ever happening to them again. And that is when they made their pact a solid promise: Divorce is not an option. They would stick to their wedding vows no matter what.

One year later, there were no regrets – only happiness.

"Sometimes, we just have to forgive and move forward," Taylor said.

And that's exactly what they did.

Learnings:

- To make a relationship or marriage work, you have to forgive people easily and often.
- Love is not a feeling but a commitment. If you can get through the bad stuff, you will be stronger as a couple and as individuals.

Kathy Lynn's Katrina Story

Lesson: *"Never take anything for granted."*
–Kathy Lynn

After leaving the company where I had worked for twenty-four years, divorcing after twenty years of marriage and starting a new relationship, I stabilized myself in New Orleans in a move I had always looked forward to making. Three years later, I found

myself in the middle of the largest disaster ever to hit the United States. In 2005, a hurricane named Katrina, which I've been told means "cleansing" in Spanish, thrust change upon a population. And change we did.

The experience of Katrina was a life-altering event whether you had damage to your house or not, whether you left or stayed. Each person was changed in some way as a result of the storm. Some were small changes; others were devastating. We are still recovering as I write this book, almost three and a half years later.

I was one of the very fortunate. With my dog and boyfriend in tow, I drove out of town Sunday at 3 a.m., about twenty-seven hours before Katrina made landfall. We started out in Florida for two weeks, then went to Virginia, where my family lives, for two weeks. We finally ended up with my best friend in Tennessee. When we started home, Hurricane Rita became a threat, so we took an unplanned detour through cities we had always wanted to visit: Charleston, South Carolina; and Savannah, Georgia. I think we were probably all in shock during those weeks away from home. It's hard to describe all the feelings I went through in those first few days.

I can remember not being able to sleep as the storm was coming ashore. I sat alone with my dog in the van, listening to the radio for hours during the night and into the early morning Monday, and again on Tuesday, trying to get news of what was going on. It was so eerie not being able to get through to anyone. All communication was lost for a period of time, and of course we all imagined the worst. My house is not far from the Mississippi River, and I imagined a forty-foot wall of water crashing down on it. (Later I would find out that my home sits on some of the highest ground in the city, and in one of the safest areas.) I also own a condo in my beloved French Quarter just across the river from my home, and I had images of the streets I'd walked so many times being under water and completely destroyed. Of course, as we all know now, the French Quarter was virtually untouched by the storm because of its location.

I was sitting in the van with my Gatsby Dog at my side when I got a confirmed report from New Orleans that the French Quarter had survived. I remember it vividly, as if it were yesterday. I sat and cried for about ten minutes straight. They were tears of joy and thankfulness that such a historic, wonderful place that so many love and call home had survived.

Later, watching the events unfold on TV was just unreal! It was like something out of a movie. I couldn't believe what was happening to my city and to the people who'd stayed behind. At that point, reality set in. After some time had passed, I was able to make a call to my neighbors and I learned that we were basically spared most of the damage. Aside from downed trees and wind damage, we were fine. There were about thirty brave souls in my neighborhood who had stayed behind, and through their daily phone calls I lived vicariously, listening to stories of looting and terror. The neighbors who stayed fed neighborhood animals and went into people's homes to rescue their dogs, cats, fish and birds. They lived in terrible conditions for weeks to protect their property and the community, and they were our heroes. Each neighborhood has its own Katrina story, and each is different. But there are heroes, happiness and sadness in all of them.

We returned to New Orleans after five weeks, and I remember getting on my bike and riding to the levee to look at the city. I cried at how lonely it looked. It was so quiet. The usual joy, music and excitement were gone. I had always loved the variety of sounds in my neighborhood: the ships on the river, the train whistle, the calliope on the paddleboat. But there were no noises drifting over the river from the French Quarter that day. Total quiet.

I also rode through my neighborhood and saw several people cleaning up branches and debris from their yards. I can remember thinking how they all seemed shell-shocked and robotic. They all seemed numbed by the experience. It reminded me of that movie where aliens inhabit the bodies of people in a town, and they look the same but definitely aren't.

I had only been back about two weeks when I decided it was time. Time to have a party! What we in New Orleans are known for! I figured, what better way to help us all try and return to some sense of normalcy? We needed to get together and talk and share our experiences. There was such a great need to be with people and just listen. That night at the party I heard so many stories, and the conversations all started the same: Did you stay or leave? When did you get out of town? Where did you go? Tell me your story, please!

It was that night that Ed, a neighbor and chef from the French Quarter, told me his story and how the experience had completely changed his life. He said he'd never look at people the same. I think that people throughout the United States who helped those from New Orleans changed our lives forever. That's when it hit me! This is why I hadn't finished my "change" book two years before the storm – because there was more change to come.

Katrina transformed my outlook on life. I had always been a positive, upbeat person but have become even more so, appreciating every day that God gives me.

Learnings:

- Never take anything for granted.
- People matter most in life.
- While material possessions don't matter, you can't help but miss special ones such as photos. After the storm, what people mentioned most were the family photos they could never replace.

- Be prepared for anything and have a plan for your family in case of a local or national disaster. Do not depend on the government to help you.
- Live life to the fullest each day, because it could be your last.

Lesson 7 Questions

Are you prepared for a natural disaster in the area where you live? Should one take place, what is the plan for your family and friends? How will you stay in touch? How will you communicate?

If you lost all of your material possessions tomorrow, what would you do and how important would they really be to you?

LESSON 8

WHEN YOU FEAR SOMETHING, DO IT

"They can conquer who believe they can."

Virgil

A Public-Speaking Nightmare

Lesson: *"I decided that the best way to bounce back was to simply try again."*

–Kenneth Graham, Ph.D., Business Consultant
Chicago

Just imagine: You're chosen to deliver a speech at your high school Christmas pageant to an auditorium packed with 1,200 parents and community members. But when it's your turn to speak, you go completely blank.

Ken Graham will never forget that moment, because it changed his life. He vividly described to me the fear that gripped him when the curtains opened and he saw all of those strangers staring at him. He was paralyzed. He simply could not speak or move.

Realizing that Ken was in trouble, a teacher ran up the stairs behind the stage, crouched behind the curtain and read each word for him to repeat. Ken said it was awful. He was embarrassed and totally destroyed by the event. He could only imagine what others thought of him after that night, and he knew it couldn't be worse than what he himself was thinking: that he was total loser.

Ken spent the weekend wondering what to do and how to conquer this fear. He decided that the best way to bounce back was to simply try again. Ken knew that he wouldn't take a forty-hour course to learn to ride a bike for the first time, and he saw public speaking in the same vein. It was something he would learn by doing. So he seized every opportunity to be in front of a group.

He began with a speech in history class in front of twenty classmates. Gradually, the more he was exposed to the experience, the less threatening it became. Eventually, he worked up the courage to deliver a speech to the entire student body, and he got through it without freezing. And while he said it wasn't anything to write home about, it was a step in the right direction.

Ken graduated the next year and entered Penn State University, where he was required to take a public speaking course. Instead of waiting until his senior year like most students, he signed up right away. The course, along with his involvement in several clubs, continued to build his confidence and poise, as well as his ability to think on his feet.

When Ken graduated he enlisted in the Army, and one of the first required training classes was a Methods of Instruction session. During the session, each person had to stand up and address his peers. Ken volunteered to go first, and when he was finished, another life-changing moment occurred. One of the group members said, "This guy sounds like he does this for a living." And that's when the light bulb went on. Ken realized that not only had he gotten over his fear of public speaking, he was actually good at it. Heck, maybe he even liked it!

After obtaining his doctorate from Penn State, Ken taught classes at both Penn State and the University of Texas. He has held leadership positions at several large companies and has been a consultant and workshop leader for several organizations. He is also a much sought-after professional speaker at conferences. From a terrified teen to a polished speaker and consultant, Ken is a great example of not only facing your fear, but using that fear to propel you to success.

Learnings:

- When you fear something in life, do it. Rather than taking a speaking course, actually speak. That's the best way to get over your fear.
- Pay attention to others who have skills that you admire.
- Success with this endeavor gave Ken confidence to try other things, and it helped shape him as a risk-taker in life.

- When you know that you might freeze up in a certain situation, have a plan for how you will handle it.

9/11 Experience Prompts Career Change

Lesson: *"Knowing who you are is the critical first step. Many people spend their whole lives figuring out who they are while they are busy going somewhere. If you know, go. If you don't know, figure it out – it may be right in front of you. Often it is much simpler and more basic than people realize."*

–Andrew Plunkett, Business Owner
Georgia

Andrew relayed to me that his life change was the decision to start his own business. It came shortly after the September 11, 2001, terrorist attacks on the World Trade Center in New York, and Andrew said his decision was spurred by his employer's response to the tragedy.

"I'm from New York and have so many friends and family who were impacted by this event," he said. "It was a dramatic experience for me."

Andrew said the head of his company sent out a heartless memo on September 12, telling employees to "get a grip and handle the event." The CEO demanded that the employees get over it and get back to work.

That memo forced Andrew to take a hard look at his situation. This was no way to treat people who had just witnessed such a horrible event. As he put it, he realized he was working at a company "without a soul."

Immediately afterward, Andrew decided to leave.

When I asked him how he was able to make such a big change so quickly, he said that he believes some people adapt more easily to change. He said it has to do with the environment in which

they're raised and how their parents react to change. His family lived in Georgia, New York and Japan, so Andrew was definitely accustomed to different life experiences. He believes that made it easier.

Andrew got through his big change by turning to friends, mentors and peers for encouragement, and he used his fear of failure as motivation. Andrew said the possibility of failure actually helped him succeed.

Faith in oneself is also crucial to successfully navigating major life change, he said. Andrew believes in being passionate about what you want to do, and says that hard work trumps luck in the business world. To have luck, he said, you need preparation and opportunity.

Learnings:

- Andrew realized he was not embracing life to the fullest. He was too conservative and was selling out rather than truly living.
- Our days are numbered, and you have to live with the decisions that you make, including the people with whom you choose to associate.
- Faith in yourself and the future helps create opportunity. Trusting in who you are and where you are going truly does make a difference.
- Knowing who you are is the critical first step. Many people spend their whole lives figuring out who they are while they are busy going somewhere. If you know, go. If you don't know, figure it out – it may be right in front of you. Often it is much simpler and more basic than people realize.
- There are second and third chances, so don't paralyze yourself with what you can't do. Instead, focus on what you can and will do.
- Failure just means you will appreciate success more.

Successful Weight-Loss Maintenance For 37 Years

Lesson: *"Don't be too hard on yourself and enjoy life along the way."*
–John Houston

John has what many people pay thousands of dollars to achieve. He lost a large amount of weight when he was young, and he has successfully kept it off for decades.

"I'm afraid I will wake up one day and be 300 pounds and no one will love me anymore," he said when I asked if he worries about gaining it back. "That fat kid is still in there, and I'm not sure I will ever get rid of him."

In first grade John was a skinny, even scrawny child, but by fourth grade he started gaining weight. By eighth grade, he had become what he calls "that fat kid," with 180 pounds on his 5-foot frame.

John said he had no friends and he didn't participate in extracurricular activities at school. He was insecure, lonely and very sad. By the beginning of his junior year in high school, he was 5 feet 7 inches tall and 232 pounds. He described himself as "a blimp with no dates and poor self-esteem."

Concerned for his happiness and his health, John's parents decided it was time to do something. They took him to their family doctor, who put him on a strict diabetic diet. His parents motivated him by giving him $2 for each pound he lost.

John took the doctor's instructions as gospel, and for the first time in a long time, he was motivated. Until now, he knew nothing about nutrition and had never eaten properly. But as he followed the diet and stayed the course, the weight began to come off slowly but surely each week.

At first, the money was his main motivation. But as people

began to notice, the money wasn't as important as the reaction he got from others and the boost to his self-esteem. During his junior year in high school, the pounds continued to melt away. Suddenly, he had friends for the first time since fourth grade. By the end of his senior year, he had reached his goal of 150 pounds.

At the time of this writing, John is fifty-three. He has maintained his weight for decades, and is living proof that the weight-loss battle can be won.

Learnings:

- John never eats junk food or fast food. He takes the time to cook his meals each day, and he grows his own vegetables.
- He tries to use the nutrition lessons and eating habits he learned in high school, and he has stuck to them, more or less, for his entire life.
- Of course, he cheats and sometimes goes over his desired weight by a few pounds, but John says the secret is to quickly get back under control.
- John's advice is don't be too hard on yourself, and enjoy life along the way.

Change Of Environment Changes Attitude

Lesson:

"People are very loving and open. We are not all that different, even though we may look different on the outside."
–Peter, Social Worker
Charleston, South Carolina

Peter was in his last year of college when he was given the opportunity to study in Buenos Aires, Argentina, for a year. He jumped at the chance, and it ended up being a major turning point in his life.

Peter was raised in an ultra-conservative farm culture in Iowa. He said he grew up in an environment where people repressed their feelings and didn't share their emotions. He described his environment as one in which he was told how to think and behave, and where the community and the church dictated what he did. Although he had loving parents, he said they taught him a negative attitude about people in general. He said his parents were always concerned about what everyone else in the community thought, and rather than making decisions based on what was right for the family or situation, they made them based on the neighbors' opinions.

It was against this backdrop that Peter's Buenos Aires experience unfolded. He realized that there was a completely different world beyond the closed-minded community he had known. He would hear news of other countries, and he became much more aware of how big the world really was. He returned to Iowa a changed man. When he joined the seminary a year later, he was sent on another journey, this time to Charleston, South Carolina.

Peter arrived in Charleston and was assigned to live in one of the poorer and predominantly African-American neighborhoods. He was used to living in an all-white community and was shocked to see mostly black faces when he got off the bus in his new neighborhood.

For the first few days, Peter said he would literally run into his house and lock every door behind him. After a couple days of this "nonsense," as he now describes it, he turned to his list. The list is a process that Peter goes through to help him make sense of major change or transition. He got out a sheet of paper and drew a line down the middle. On one side he wrote down all of the things he liked about Charleston; the other side was devoted to why he hated it and should leave immediately. The positives won. Peter promptly unlocked his door, poured a glass of wine and went out to sit on his

front porch.

Within a week, Peter had more friends (most of them African-American) than he ever dreamed. He came to realize that we are all just people with the same challenges and the same ups and downs, regardless of race.

Learnings:

- Peter learned that most people are very loving and open, and that we are not that different from one another, even though we may look different on the outside.
- He learned how important it is to create an open environment where people can express their true feelings.
- He learned to relate to people in a positive way, and to find the good in people instead of focusing on their faults.
- He learned to use his "list" process when making major decisions and changes.

If I Had It To Do Over, I Probably Wouldn't Change A Thing

Lesson: *"My favorite learning is once you know it's time to move on, just do it. Don't be afraid to take that leap, and don't stay around just for the money. Happiness is more important than money."*

–Kathy Lynn

I was a successful executive with a Fortune 100 Company running an $850 million division. After twenty-four years, I suddenly asked myself: Is this all there is? Work, making money and stress? I was giving my all to others and to the organization, but I had no time for my family or myself. I was totally consumed by the daily duties of my job, rushing headlong to nowhere. I wasn't unhappy, but something was missing. I asked myself: What is my purpose in life? Isn't there more than this?

Are you familiar with the "stages of change" for organizations and companies? It begins with the start-up stage, then the growth stage, followed by maturity and then decline, or reinvention and change. One day it hit me: Life is like that, too. We move from the infant stage through youth to young adult. In our twenties and thirties we are growing and shaping ourselves, then maturity begins in our forties and fifties, followed by a decline or self-reinvention. Is that why some people in their eighties seem much younger, while others seem much older? I think it is. It's how we react to the changes in life that makes the difference. Our choices. The changes we choose to make and the choices we make about the changes we encounter.

After leaving the corporate world, I felt my true self begin to emerge. During those corporate years, I never felt like the real me. I was always trying to be the "perfect woman" – whatever that was. It was tough being one of the first females in a management position at my company. I was in the male-dominated area of sales, which was even tougher, but I was successful at it. I also had lots of great guys encouraging, coaching and helping me along the way.

I molded myself into the woman who wanted to get ahead, and it worked. I changed my hairstyle and the way I dressed. I joined the right organizations. But I drew the line when one boss suggested that I take speech classes to get rid of my very Southern Virginia accent. Is it any wonder that I lost a little of who I was during it all? I was very successful in the corporate world for many years, but I lost a little of myself in the process. I made a lot of money, but I lost a little of my soul along the way.

And guess what? If had a chance to do it all over again, I probably wouldn't change a thing! I was learning at the time where women stood in the workforce. I had far more positive experiences

than negative ones, and I also learned a lot through great advice from others and from various public speaking and motivational courses. And I had great coaches. So I wouldn't trade my years in the corporate world at all. I grew and learned lessons that helped me later in life.

I have since started my own consulting business and have become an author and public speaker. It was not easy making the change, and it has taken me about five years to get my income back to my previous level. But it has been worth it, and I've had fun along the way. I now live full-time in the city I've always dreamed of, and I wake up feeling blessed every day. I love what I do, and my life is rich with great friends and neighbors! I have found my home, my purpose and my place in life.

Learnings:

- Once you know it's time to move on with something, just do it – move on. Don't be afraid or stay around for the money. It's easy to do when you are making a six-figure income, but in the long run, it's not worth it. Life is short. Happiness is more important than money.
- Make contacts outside your company. We all get so involved with work that one day we wake up and realize that everyone we know – all our friends — are at the company where we work every day. That's not healthy. It's great to have relationships and contacts outside of work, so that when you are ready to make a change, you have other resources you can turn to for help.
- Be part of the community. I was working crazy hours and believed that I was already involved with plenty of good causes through my job. Get involved with one or two good organizations outside of work. Not only will you contribute to the community you live in, you will make good friends and establish interests outside your occupation.
- Go for it. We all have a God-given natural talent. Find yours and use it. That will bring you happiness.

Lessons 8 Questions

What is it that you fear in life?

What steps can you take to confront your fears?

LESSON 9

TOOLS AND TECHNIQUES FOR CHANGE

"When you were born, you cried and the world rejoiced. Live your life so that when you die, the world cries and you rejoice."

Cherokee Proverb

Tools And Techniques For Change

- Take action. Don't just think about it – do it!
- Take time to know yourself. Take a retreat and focus on what you want in life.
- Help others with the things they are trying to change. Learning from their experiences may make your own changes easier to handle.
- Practice patience. Sometimes change occurs slowly.
- Understand that everything in life happens for a reason. This allows you to see unforeseen changes in a new light.
- Reach out to others when you're going through a change. Share ideas and experiences with others in similar situations.
- Pray and meditate daily.
- Read books about the change that you want to make in your life.
- Attend workshops on change.
- Take a community college course that applies to the change you want to make.
- To avoid feeling overwhelmed, take small steps toward the change you seek.
- Create a network of people outside your usual contacts so that when you need to change, you have other resources to tap.
- Be an active member of your community. Meet people and help them through changes.
- Natural disasters can occur anywhere. Formulate a plan for you and your family.
- Take time each day to nurture your spirituality.
- Engage a counselor to help you overcome your fear of change.

Master List Of The Learnings By Story

Amanda Overmyer, page 22

- Amanda says her decision to try her luck on "American Idol" gave her the opportunity to pursue her music career – an opportunity she wouldn't have had if she hadn't taken the chance.
- Always be yourself and stay true to your convictions.
- No matter what you want to do or change – go for it. It's not the end of the world if it doesn't turn out exactly like you wanted.
- It is better to have tried than to look back when you are older and realize you never took a chance on what you wanted in life.
- Frequently choose to take the road less traveled – we only live once.
- If you have changes you would like to make in life, make them. The only thing that can stop you is...you.

Andrew Plunkett, page 134

- Andrew realized he was not embracing life to the fullest. He was too conservative and was selling out rather than truly living.
- Our days are numbered, and you have to live with the decisions that you make, including the people with whom you choose to associate.
- Faith in yourself and the future helps create opportunity. Trusting in who you are and where you are going truly does make a difference.
- Knowing who you are is the critical first step. Many people spend their whole lives figuring out who they are while they are busy going somewhere. If you know, go. If you don't know, figure it out – it may be right in front of you. Often it is much simpler and more basic than people realize.
- There are second and third chances, so don't paralyze yourself with what you can't do. Instead, focus on what you can and will do.
- Failure just means you will appreciate success more.

Angela Cryer, page 2

- Angela learned patience and forgiveness. If she gets mad now, she gets over it quickly. Life is too short, and tomorrow is not promised.
- It is possible for relationships to grow stronger in the face of adversity. Angela's marriage has grown, and she and her husband have grown as friends. They say I love you more often and call each other several times a day just to say hello.
- Angela grew spiritually and learned the value of volunteering and helping others. She remembers how she was helped, and vowed to give back.
- Angela has learned not to make excuses. Don't put anything off. Don't wait until tomorrow, because tomorrow may not come. Truly live in the moment.
- No "woulda, coulda, shoulda" in Angela's book anymore. Just do it!

B.B. St. Roman, page 5

- Three things matter most in life: wisdom – understanding what life is about and how you fit in and set your priorities; compassion – showing feeling and respect for others; and joy – inner contentment that leads to the outer expression of happiness.
- It is possible to get along with very few material comforts, as B.B. learned by living in a Himalayan village and in many other locations around the world.
- Patience is a great virtue, especially in situations beyond your control. One might as well enjoy the situation instead of getting upset about it. Traveling to other countries around the world teaches patience quickly!
- Resilience is important – knowing how much you can endure and stretching that boundary further.
- Learn to go with the flow, knowing that everything happens for a reason and at the right time, even if we don't immediately understand it.
- Accept what you have in life and enjoy it.
- Draw from nature to be resourceful. B.B. learned resourcefulness from watching the villagers in the Himalayas work in harmony with their surroundings. There was no calendar with days of the week,

so the moon was used to mark the passing of days. Distance was measured in the days it took to walk somewhere.

- The rhythms of nature are all around us. We can see them in our own backyard if we simply take the time to look.

Blaine Kern, "Mr. Mardi Gras," page 14

- He learned from and inherited his father's talent for storytelling. Storytelling is part of being creative and passing life's lessons to the next generation.
- Cultivate the Taurus spirit of never giving up on any task you undertake – business or personal.
- Keep a positive attitude and have enthusiasm for everything you do.
- Stay physically active. Drink in moderation.
- Be able to laugh at yourself.
- Find what you were meant to do in life and pursue it relentlessly.

Carolina Gallop, page 42

- Carolina said she now realizes how important it is to spend quality time with her family. She said she had been busy living life, and assumed that her siblings would always be there. After losing her brother, she realized she had neglected that relationship. She now takes time to visit her siblings frequently. The loss of her brother brought her closer to the rest of her family, and also to her husband.
- Never take life for granted.
- Reaching out to others in times of grief is the best remedy, especially when you connect with those who have experienced similar loss.

Cathy Gaudet, page 44

- Live for today. We are not promised tomorrow.
- Make a list of the things you want to do before you die and do it!
- Family and friendships are what are really important in life.

- Trust that God has a plan.

Charles Gillam, page 98

- Be persistent; don't let anything hold you back from trying to do what you want to do.
- Try to do the right things, and be careful about what you ask God for. You usually get it, and you need to be alert when it comes.
- When things happen in your life, they are all connected. Let your life flow, and the right things will usually happen.
- Be honest and loyal to others and to yourself.
- Treat people the way you want to be treated. Remember that love always conquers hate.
- Leave something behind for others.

Connie and Claudius Fincher, with Flea, page 80

- You must put your complete faith in God. Everything is transient; nothing lasts forever.
- The love of God works through people.
- Connie and Claudius learned how to be more tolerant of other people, and they developed an inner peace from the experience.
- It doesn't pay to get upset about things that you can't take with you.
- When you hear that a storm is coming, get out!
- Connie learned from her guardian angel, Patty, that there are wonderful people in this world who give selflessly. Patty was not afraid, even when Connie was. She just moved forward and helped people. God worked through Patty, and gave her the confidence to do what she did.

Elaine, page 24

- Be true to yourself.
- Sometimes it's ok to be selfish and to take care of yourself first.

Fay Faron, page 114

- Take on change in manageable bites. Consider one problem at a time and figure out how to solve it to be happy.
- When Fay found herself going through tough times, she made up a phrase that she always goes back to when approaching change in her life: "This is who I am now and what I do."
- Fay credits her parents for giving her the love and security that fostered her can-do attitude.
- Look for the up side of loss. What positive can come out of it?

Fritz Harsdorff, page 117

- Poverty can lead a person into making poor choices. But opportunity and the means to do better can change his or her life forever.
- Military service teaches responsibility and instills self-confidence.
- In leaving home and experiencing the wider world, we become more open as human beings.

Hillery Moise, page 26

- Don't be ashamed if everything isn't perfect in your life; we are all human, and it's ok to be human.
- Don't live according to the expectations of others.
- Don't try to fix others. You can only fix yourself.
- If you think you have a problem that can't be solved, just wait until tomorrow. Everything looks different after a night's sleep.
- Don't get so caught up in trying to make everything go the way you think it should. Allow things to run their natural course.

Hollie Vest, "Almost-Tina Turner," page 100

- Hollie said she will always love to sing and entertain people and make them happy. Performing is in her blood, and it's what she loves to do best. She is happiest when on stage.
- Hollie has learned that privacy is also important to her. Performing

as a character or doing tribute shows allows her both the peace of privacy and the pleasure of performing.

- Don't take yourself too seriously and never lose your sense of humor. A sense of humor is the best medicine, especially during hard times.
- Perseverance, persistence and resilience are important qualities, no matter what your goals and career demand of you.
- It's important to learn how to overcome obstacles and make a way when you think there is no way. Don't think about what you can't do. Think about what is possible. Out of horrible things, wonderful things can happen.
- Never lose faith or give up on what you believe in or what is truly your heart's desire.
- From Hurricane Katrina, Hollie learned that things are replaceable or reparable. It taught her that family and friends mean everything.
- Cherish those you love and protect them as best you can.
- Show kindness to someone every day. Even small acts of kindness can change someone's life.
- Don't be afraid to do something you have never done before. That is how we grow, become stronger and wise.
- Cultivate your purpose. Have a reason to be excited about waking up every morning, even if it's simply doing the very best you can with whatever it is you're doing.

James, page 119

- It's important to get professional coaching and psychological help when going through a serious illness.
- Remove as much stress from your life as you can, even if it means ending a relationship, quitting your job or whatever it takes to find peace.
- Learn all you can about your illness, and be assertive with your doctors.
- Truly live in the moment. Travel and enjoy your life.
- Friends who accept you as you are are greater than any treasure. Give back to them.

Jane, page 10

- Jane learned that we are all connected as a community. She realized that everyone who experienced Hurricane Katrina lost something because of the way we are all connected.
- Stay in the present and savor the moment.
- Give people your full attention and respect.
- Get angry and let it out, but don't wallow.
- Lose the guilt in your life, whatever it is.

Jerry, page 84

- Jerry's religion kept her focused and gave her purpose in life.
- She learned to rely on her faith in her husband, knowing that he was faithful and waiting for her, just as she was waiting for him.
- A hang-in-there attitude kept her going while her husband was away at war. She kept busy, knowing that their separation would eventually end.
- Trust yourself and the person you love.
- Loneliness is a burden. Surround yourself with friends of all ages.

Jo and Fritz Harsdorff, page 12

- You have to work at marriage to keep it strong.
- Be tolerant of your partner's faults.
- Make a commitment to the marriage, and no matter what, work it out. If one person is down, the other picks up the slack. Be a constant best friend and partner.
- Love and respect one another at all times.
- Become comfortable with each other.
- Separate bedrooms are a must. This arrangement allows each person privacy and space.
- Too much togetherness is a blow to any marriage. You must have freedom and absolute trust.

- A sense of humor is essential.
- It's important to truly like each other as friends.
- Love where you live.

John, page 136

- John doesn't eat junk food or fast food. He takes the time to cook his meals each day, and he grows his own vegetables.
- He tries to use the nutrition lessons and eating habits he learned in high school, and he has stuck to them, more or less, for his entire life.
- Of course, he cheats and sometimes goes over his desired weight by a few pounds, but John says the secret is to quickly get back under control.
- John's advice is don't be too hard on yourself, and enjoy life along the way.

Jon Racherbaumer, page 103

- One of our most important assets is our psychic equipoise or balance. We have to be like tightrope walkers in life. Life changes, such as job loss or relationship problems, can throw us out of balance for a time, and it is important to know how to work through the changes quickly.
- Jon said times of upheaval are opportunities to reconsider and reassess our lives.
- When you go through a change that is forced upon you, look for the opportunity it presents rather than focus on the loss.
- Most people fear change. Be willing to take risks and test your strengths and weaknesses.
- Jon said he has learned more from his failures than from his successes. Don't be afraid to fail.
- Learn to appreciate mystery for its power to energize us and keep us curious about ourselves and the world around us. Embrace the wonder of not knowing.

Kathy Lynn

Purpose, page 16

- Listen to what people say you are good at. It may reveal your life purpose.
- Welcome life changes. There is a master plan for each of us, and by changing we are getting closer to what we are meant to do.

Love, page 32

- Don't react too quickly. Give yourself time to make sure what you are feeling is the real thing.
- On the flip side, don't be afraid to change if it is the real thing. I believe my husband and I were meant to be together for those years we shared, and I still love him. He is one of my best friends, but we had to go through the messy and nasty divorce stuff that most people go through in order to get there. My piano entertainer was meant to come into my life at that time to help me on to the next part of my journey. We were together six years, but it was not a bed of roses.
- Have your finances in order and always make sure you know what your financial status is, man or woman. One person should not handle all the finances in a marriage. Be informed.
- Draw up a prenuptial agreement if you need one. Get divorced in the right state! Know the laws.
- Try to work things out as much as you can, and use the same attorney if you can to save money and feelings.
- I believe divorce is simply the right thing for some couples. Marriage is not for everyone.
- Be happy and live the life you are meant to live. Sometimes, you have to make the tough choices.
- I truly believe that people come and go in our lives exactly when they are meant to. There is a bigger plan for each of us…we just have to be open to it.
- I think some people are actually happier being single and surrounding themselves with friends, family and special romances.
- If you fall in love…go for it. You only live once.

Loss, page 51

- At the toughest times in our lives, friends and community are so important in helping us deal with our grief.
- Even if you think you spend enough time with someone you love, spend more time while you can. Enjoy them every day, every moment that God allows. Tell them you love them every day. You can never tell someone enough how important they are.
- Talk to loved ones about death. Don't feel awkward – it's part of life.
- You need friends to get through the tough times. Lean on them, and give back to them when they need you.
- Don't just trust what the doctors say. Look for alternative treatments and learn from others about what has worked for them.

Gatsby, page 71

- At the toughest times in our lives, friends and community are so important in helping us deal with our grief.
- Out of something sad can come something good if we look for something bigger than ourselves.
- God does answer prayers when we have faith.

Spirituality, page 93

- Make time for yourself and your spirituality every day.
- Meditation helps refocus your day.
- When we use our learnings to help others, we are blessed because we become stronger ourselves.

Health, page 107

- There is no perfect body. It is better to be strong and healthy than to look like the skinny models that magazines tell us we should look like.
- The old adage of a balanced diet really works when combined with strength training and cardio work.
- Try not to obsess over weight. Enjoy life and stay active.
- Try different aerobic exercises such as biking and roller blading to keep your workouts interesting.

- Get an exercise partner who goes to the gym every day. It will motivate you to show up and not let them down.
- Reading books on fitness and exercise helps me stay focused on being fit.

Katrina, page 124

- Never take anything for granted.
- People matter most in life.
- While material possessions don't matter, you can't help but miss special ones such as photos. After the storm, what people mentioned most were the family photos they could never replace.
- Be prepared for anything and have a plan for your family in case of a local or national disaster. Do not depend on the government to help you.
- Live life to the fullest each day, because it could be your last.

Career, page 139

- Once you know it's time to move on with something, just do it – move on. Don't be afraid or stay around for the money. It's easy to do when you are making a six-figure income, but in the long run, it's not worth it. Life is short. Happiness is more important than money.
- Make contacts outside your company. We all get so involved with work that one day we wake up and realize that everyone we know – all of our friends – are at the company where we work every day. That's not healthy. It's great to have relationships and contacts outside of work, so that when you are ready to make a change, you have other resources you can turn to for help.
- Be part of the community. I was working crazy hours and believed that I was already involved with plenty of good causes through my job. Get involved with one or two good organizations outside of work. Not only will you contribute to the community you live in, you will make good friends and establish interests outside your occupation.
- Go for it. We all have a God-given natural talent. Find yours and use it. That will bring you happiness.

Ken Graham

Father, page 66

- Whatever you do in life, make sure to put people first.
- Everyone has an important role to play in life. It's how we treat each other in these roles that makes the difference.

Public Speaking, page 132

- When you fear something in life, do it. Rather than taking a speaking course, actually speak. That is the best way to get over your fear.
- Pay attention to others who have skills that you admire.
- Success with this endeavor gave Ken confidence to try other things, and it helped shape him as a risk-taker in life.
- When you know that you might freeze up in a certain situation, have a plan for how to handle it.

Lily, page 48

- In order to think, we must take time for ourselves with no interruptions. At the retreat, Lily learned to make this a part of her daily life. Now, for half an hour each morning, she spends time reflecting on God and reading spiritual works. She said this gets her focused and centered for the day.

Ms. Irene Burrus

Living, page 68

- Do everything in moderation: eating, drinking, TV, exercise, gambling. Don't let anything become an addiction.
- Have friends of all ages, and make sure they are diverse in every way. You learn more from people who are different from you.
- Be part of many different clubs and organizations that have diverse memberships.
- Choose a life partner whom you respect and who will give you your space to do what you want in life.
- Stay informed. Read newspapers and magazines, listen to smart

people and learn from them, and watch educational shows on TV to keep your mind active.

- Don't turn your business affairs over to someone else. The more involved you are and the more responsibility you maintain, the better your mental health.
- Have enthusiasm for life.
- Stay interested in everything around you, from the environment to politics.
- Live each day to the fullest.
- Make friends with people you respect. They will influence your quality of life.
- Stay active.
- Eat right.
- Don't waste time worrying about things you can't control, but make an impact where you can.
- Live within your means so that your money can last and you can remain independent.

Loss, page 121

- Life can change so quickly! It's not smooth. We all have tragedies in our lives.
- Appreciate your relationships. Ms. Irene said she was truly blessed to have been close to her daughter for years.

Marcia Ensley, page 86

- Take charge of your own medical care; ask questions and demand answers of the people treating you.
- Ask friends for referrals to better care if you don't feel comfortable with your doctors.
- Find a support system, even if it's an Internet blog.
- Lean on your faith. Understand that there is a master plan, and go with it.

Michelle Toca, page 29

- Just do it – whatever it is in your life that you have been waiting to do.
- Be happy with yourself. Don't feel guilty about pursuing your dreams.
- Don't conform to what society or other people expect. Be yourself.
- If you are confident in yourself and respectful of other people, you will receive that in return most of the time.
- Be helpful to others. You can make an impact on others' lives just by taking the time to do a kind thing.
- Try to really listen and understand people.
- Accept yourself for who you are. Once you do, you can accept others and be happy. It's a wonderful life out there – go find it!

Olivia Foret, page 40

- When you go through tough times in your life, you learn who your real friends are.
- Olivia said when she experiences hard times, she turns to God for strength. She said her faith in God can see her through anything.
- Self-worth comes from being proud of who you are. Be proud of yourself and your body no matter what size you are or shape you are in. Carve out the time to take care of yourself.
- Only by taking care of yourself can you be at your best for those you love.
- Health is vital for living your life to the fullest. You need to be the best you can be physically and mentally.
- Honesty and self-worth are crucial to happiness. All else will follow if you put God first and your family second, and be honest and take care of yourself.

Pam Irvin, page 49

- The things that helped her through her career change were daily yoga, meditation, and reading self-help books. Her favorite book

is *You Can Heal Your Life* by Louise Hay. Pam also met with a counselor to talk about her fear. The talks led her to the realization that her fear of change was irrational. Change is a constant in the universe.

- Pam feels there are specific lessons that each person's life reveals. She said we are guided to these lessons, but it's up to us to have the courage to accept and learn them. Self-awareness – knowing who you are and being at peace with that knowledge – makes the journey a lot easier. Some say that only 5 percent of us will ever achieve such a level of self-awareness. Her advice to others? Feel the fear and do it anyway!

Paul Longo, page 89

- Paul's change led to the discovery of internal resources and an awareness of both the teacher and the student inside him.
- He learned to cherish questions more than answers. He said the formation of a good question gets your heart and soul involved in the process.
- He learned the difference between emptiness and fullness, and said sometimes it is better to be empty.
- People feel trapped when they are not thinking creatively. Use logic and every available resource to find options.
- Hope and love are both nouns and verbs; faith is only a noun. Does that mean there's nothing to do when it comes to having faith? No, go back to loving and hoping more, and your faith will grow.

Peter, page 137

- Peter learned that most people are very loving and open, and that and we are not that different from one another, even though we may look different on the outside.
- He learned how important it is to create an open environment where people can express their true feelings.
- He learned to relate to people in a positive way, and to find the good in people instead of focusing on their faults.
- He learned to use his "list" process when making major decisions and changes.

Philippart and Anja, page 105

- Keep an open mind, especially to people from other countries. Respect their values and learn why they do things the way they do.
- If you have no prejudices, you will have a richer life. Then the world becomes a treasure chest – dive in and you can get as rich as you want!
- Spend time communicating with and trying to understand your partner. Keeping an open mind is the foundation of a successful relationship.
- Don't be afraid to change. Most people are afraid to get out of their box.

Polly, page 90

- Steve's death allowed Polly to learn how to accept help from others – not financial help, but small things like someone picking up the kids or dropping off a cooked meal. Polly had always felt she should be self-sufficient, but Steve's passing made her realize how important it is to accept kindness from others and to be there for others when they are in need.
- Going from a partnership to being a single parent is tough, but it can be done. The most important thing is to make sure you are there for your children, teaching them and helping them to cope – especially during the early years.
- Don't settle for the easy choices. Ask yourself what is the right thing to do and do it, even if it's tough and people criticize you.

Taylor, page 120

- To make a relationship or marriage work, you have to forgive people easily and often.
- Love is not a feeling but a commitment. If you can get through the bad stuff, you will be stronger as a couple and as individuals.

Vinnie Pervel, page 60

- It's ok to accept things from people without feeling embarrassed.

- The most important thing in life is helping others.
- If you expect something in return for doing good, you will be disappointed.
- If you don't expect anything in return for helping others, and you get something anyway, it is a double blessing.

Yvonne Sharpe, page 58

- There is something in the world greater than you. The earlier we learn it, the better off we are.
- People are happier when they focus on the bigger world outside of themselves.
- Learn to ask yourself: "What do you want your gravestone to say about your life?" This will give you a sharp focus on what you do each and every day.
- Learn to judge people as individuals instead of grouping them in categories.

Lesson 9 Questions

Imagine at your funeral that several of your friends are speaking about you, and all of them say that you really knew how to live your life to the fullest. Describe what they are talking about.

Where are you today in relation to the above description?

What steps can you take to get there in the next year?

Order Form

To order additional books, please visit:
www.kathylynn.net
or Fax to: 504-367-6324
or Postal order to:
Gatsby Consulting • 301 Delaronde Street
New Orleans, LA 70114

NAME: ____________________

ADDRESS: ____________________

____

____

____

PHONE NUMBER: ____________________

E-MAIL: ____________________

QUANTITY: ____________________

BOOK PRICE: ____________________

SALES TAX: ____________________

SHIPPING: ____________________

TOTAL PAYMENT AMOUNT: ____________________

To inquire about Kathy Lynn's public speaking engagements, contact Gatsby Consulting at www.kathylynn.net or call 504-367-6915.

www.ingramcontent.com/pod-product-compliance
Ingram Content Group UK Ltd.
Pitfield, Milton Keynes, MK11 3LW, UK
UKHW041945190726
13854UKWH00004B/1795